SCREEN CAPTURED

SCREEN CAPTURED

HELPING FAMILIES EXPLORE THE DIGITAL
WORLD IN THE AGE OF MANIPULATION

SEAN HERMAN

LIONCREST
PUBLISHING

SCREEN CAPTURED

Helping Families Explore the Digital World
in the Age of Manipulation

ISBN   978-1-5445-0377-6 *Hardcover*
       978-1-5445-0376-9 *Paperback*
       978-1-5445-0375-2 *Ebook*
       978-1-5445-0522-0 *Audiobook*

To my daughter Kaylie: you were the inspiration for this book,
and you continue to inspire me to be better every single day.

CONTENTS

FOREWORD

The digital world holds much promise in informing, upskilling, and empowering future generations to solve some of the world's biggest problems: climate change, universal education access, conflict prevention, and food and water security. Technology can facilitate experiential learning, connection, collaboration, and creation on an unprecedented and ever-evolving scale. However, caregivers and educators are faced with the challenge of helping children to harness the strengths of the online cosmos while avoiding the perils. It is imperative that youth resist the urge to use social media metrics ("likes" and "follows") as signposts of their self-worth and belonging, refrain from feeling that they are not 'pretty enough,' 'rich enough,' 'popular enough,' or 'talented enough' when viewing highly curated posts by their idols and be mindful of the possible future impact of the digital footprint that they are leaving today.

In this book, Sean Herman provides caregivers with a roadmap to guide their children in understanding and safely navigating this social media space. Sean draws on his own lived experience as a dad and tech industry expert, together with latest findings from psychological theories, neuroscience, interdisciplinary research, expert opinion, and mainstream media publications to present a concise yet comprehensive summary of key considerations and recommendations for helping children to confidently and successfully explore the digital world that surrounds them.

As a child and adolescent psychologist and researcher who specializes in technology, I highly recommend this book to caregivers who wish to develop a family culture characterized by calm, open communication; trust; and mutual enjoyment and discovery of the digital landscape. As Albert Einstein once said, *"The human spirit must prevail over technology."* May the force be with you!

BY DR. RENAE BEAUMONT,
CHILD AND ADOLESCENT PSYCHOLOGIST

INTRODUCTION

At age seven, my daughter changed my life with the tap of a button.

It was a morning in September. We were just hanging around the house, and my daughter, Kaylie, was in the living room on her favorite chair. She was playing with an old iPhone 6 we'd passed down to her, and she was on a new app she'd just discovered the day before. The app was called PopJam.

Looking over her shoulder, I tried not to photobomb as she took a selfie. She played with the filters, pasting familiar characters over her face, and she added stickers and text to her new creation. It looked fun: it was colorful and polished, and there were so many different animals and figures Kaylie could put in her design. She could draw all over it in a rainbow of colors. Being in the tech industry myself, I was envious of the feature set.

Kaylie settled on a picture of herself, with a dog face overlaid, wearing sunglasses and a hat. She added a sticker of a little girl, another of Captain Underpants, and a howling wolf with a unicorn horn. She added a speech bubble that said, "Ruff!"

She hit post. Almost instantly, my daughter's playful exploration filled me with confusion and concern.

Within seconds, feedback started coming in.

Great 1st creation! Have you tried the daily challenge yet? If you win, you'll get tons of followers!

PopJam liked your post!

RUFF

Great 1st creation! Have you tried the Daily Challenge yet? If you win you'll get tons of Followers!

She got a notification that she had two new followers on her public account. The first was labeled as a Staffer (I presume a PopJam staff), and the second was from an account labeled "PopJam."

She was so proud. "Daddy!" she screamed. "PopJam is following me!"

My daughter was elated. Her eyes lit up as she saw the automatic responses of PopJam engage with her and "like" her content. She got an immediate contact high from the instant gratification. (When we dive into the brain chemicals behind social media in chapter 2, you'll see I mean this literally.)

She was blissful and happy. I was disturbed.

The problem was, virtually none of this attention came from real people, or especially from anyone she knew. The app used what I assumed to be bots to give instantaneous feedback and gratification for her post. Since I was brainstorming my own app design, I was beginning to become aware of issues around dopamine and addiction that were topics of conversation in the context of social media. I was learning that this kind of attention could be toxic to developing brains. Watching my daughter's reaction to these supposed bots, something didn't sit right with me.

I latched onto that phrase: *If you win, you'll get tons of followers!*

Did I really want that for my daughter?

The responses from PopJam didn't seem to come from real people. And whether they were real or not, did I want my daughter to grow up wanting these kinds of rewards? In the span of a few seconds, the app had taught her that amassing "likes" and followers—none of whom she knew personally—meant she was important. Did I really want her monetizing the idea of followers, and chasing validation?

In this one moment, I got very curious about what kinds of interactions she would have online, and how that would shape her brain, her mental health, and her life. I needed to learn more.

CREATING SAFE ENGAGEMENT

Like many parents, I embrace tech, and I know it's here to stay. I want to teach my daughter how to safely engage with the online world. Yet here was an app, supposedly designed for kids, that was teaching her other lessons about how to engage online—and how people engage with each other.

Apps that focus on amassing "friends," followers, and "likes" are specifically designed to maximize user engagement. Developers create interesting features that are designed to not only bring more people to the app, but to keep us coming back. Built-in features teach us how to engage with and get attention from other users, and they leverage our brain chemistry and behavior to desire more "likes" and followers. They encourage users to "like" other people's posts and feed into a validation loop that can become addictive. As we'll see in later chapters, this has ripple effects for our psyche, our mental health, and our conception of self-worth.

What's more, this is affecting children at all stages of development as younger and younger users come online. As I began to consider these issues in developing my own app for families, I came across some staggering statistics from Common Sense Media:[1]

- By 2017, 98 percent of 0- to 8-year-olds had daily access to a mobile device, up from 52 percent in 2011.
- 45 percent of 0- to 8-year-olds had their own mobile device, up from 3 percent in 2011.
- 0- to 8-year-olds averaged 2 hours, 19 minutes of screen time per day in 2017.
- The proportion of leisure time children spent on mobile devices rose from 4 percent in 2011 to 35 percent in 2017, mostly at the expense of TV (which fell from 51 percent to 42 percent), DVDs (which fell from 23 percent to 12 percent), and video game systems (which fell from 10 percent to 4 percent).

---

1   "The Common Sense Census: Media Use by Kids Age Zero to Eight," *Common Sense Media,* 2017.

Percentage of 0 to 8 Year Olds With

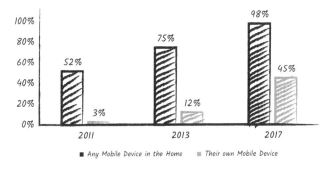

In concert with these statistics, the Common Sense Census noted that "parents are far more likely to say media helps rather than hurts their child's learning, creativity, social skills and focus." Tech isn't *coming*—it's *here*. The rise of tech has come with a lot of positive benefits, and as with anything, it's not without its risks.

Online media can be an additive or a destructive experience for kids. This book arose from my desire to understand more deeply how online behaviors affect our children, and how parents can have skillful conversations with our children about how to navigate the online world. Full disclosure: I am leading a company that is building a messenger for kids and families, but this book is not about that. My mission arose from a desire to create a safer online environment for children, and my quest to learn how to do that ultimately led me to create this book, to share what I learned with fellow parents who are helping their children safely navigate the digital world.

This book is not a step-by-step guide for how to moderate your children's online exploration—each child and each parental relationship is far too unique and complex for a prescriptive approach.

In this book, you'll find a comprehensive background to understand what is happening to our children's brains, social lives, and well-being as they "like," follow, share, and friend. We're hardwired to belong in groups, and in the early chapters of this book we'll discuss how our social networks impacted us before the rise of social media, and how the internet has made social validation far more accessible.

From there, we'll dig into the chemical components of what happens in our brains as we engage with social media, and how apps gamify our biological responses to keep us online. In later chapters, we'll discuss how app design is impacting our children's behaviors, how apps use the data they collect from our engagement, and what this means for younger and younger users who are interacting online.

We'll draw the distinction between *screen time*—which can be characterized by explorative play—and *manipulation time*, which can make young users especially vulnerable to marketing and brand agendas. I coined the term "screen captured" to refer to anytime we are being manipulated by algorithms, apps, and platforms. As you'll see in this book, we're often screen captured without realizing it. But to guide our kids to healthy online interactions, it's important to raise our awareness. In the last chapter, we'll discuss how parents can begin age-appropriate discussions with children about online activity, and tips for cultivating healthy behaviors online.

Armed with this knowledge, you'll be able to see your children's online activities with more clarity, and open discussions that help them explore the online world in a healthy and safe way.

TALKING ABOUT TECH

After seeing my daughter's reaction to attention on the PopJam app, we started a conversation about what was really going on in the app and what that meant to her. I explained that the comments she'd received weren't from real people, but from computers. These interactions weren't authentic, and they weren't truly meaningful. At age seven, this news didn't bother her nearly as much as I would have hoped; she had just been excited about the attention. I told her I wanted her to focus on real interactions with real people she cared about.

We also talked about what she liked in the app. I discovered that what she liked most was the creative aspect of transforming her photo and using stickers and other design features. With my guidance, Kaylie has switched to other apps—like Animal Jam and Minecraft—where she can play, create, build, and engage with friends as she explores the online world.

The interactions our children have online create lasting impressions and values that they take to the real world. The purpose of this book is to help you turn a critical lens on the seemingly innocent behaviors we engage in online, so that you can guide your children to healthy choices.

BUILDING BETTER APPS FOR KIDS

The first platform I worked on wasn't for kids—it was for businesses. I put my background in marketing, corporate finance, and consultation into a business-to-business video sharing app. Rather than using social media tactics of broadcasting from one user to a wider audience, the platform was designed to move video within private networks. It was meant for video messaging between individuals in a tight, private circle.

In the early startup days, our team was plugging along with development, looking for a product-market fit. We were testing it with commercial and residential real estate companies, sales organizations, and anyone we thought could benefit from using video assets instead of text in their private conversations.

That's when we noticed something interesting. One person was using the app a lot more than anyone else: they had shared more videos and engaged with the app's features more than any other user.

Guess who the user was: my (then) seven-year-old daughter.

She had been playing with the app, and she loved using the video features. She'd initially started playing with the app by onboarding her family—me, my wife, and then her grandparents—and using the app to send us videos. Then she told a few close friends at school about it, and before long they had gone home to their parents and asked them to download the app and set it up. We had just moved from Calgary to Vancouver, and as Kaylie made new friends, she was onboarding new friends onto the platform. Suddenly there were a few kids connected on our app, sharing video back and forth.

A little while later, I jolted awake at two in the morning with an epiphany: *we've got to do something like this for kids and families.*

I couldn't go back to sleep. Instead, I got up and wrote

the entire business plan for what would become Kinzoo that night. My quest to understand the apps kids were using, and the effects that particular features had on their development, began in full force. As I've learned more about how manipulation techniques in apps affect us, I've poured that knowledge into my own app design—and into this book.

I named the app Kinzoo—which combines the words kinship and zoo—because a zoo is such an apt metaphor for how we can introduce our kids to the online world. When our children want to learn about wild animals, we don't take them out into the wild. Instead, we take them to a zoo that has the right structures in place to keep them safe. In this protected environment, children can navigate themselves around, and explore more freely.

Similarly, it's important to develop the structures kids need to explore the online environment that they're growing up within. We'll learn later in the book that a majority of apps that are appealing to children (only some of which are specifically designed for kids) aren't properly motivated to put up those structures. So, the structure for a child's exploration needs to come from parents, who should educate themselves to make the distinction between healthy screen time and being screen captured. Let's face it: our kids will be on tech eventually (and the stats—and smell test—show that usership is definitely trending younger), so it is more important than ever that parents are armed to be great digital mentors.

As Jordan Shapiro writes in *The New Childhood: Raising Kids to Thrive in a Connected World*:[2]

> Every online game represents a chance to try out new ways of being with digital tools. That's a good thing, because the future is already here. We're all living in a connected world. And today's kids will need to be prepared to participate in a global economy that mediates transactions and communications through microchips and fiber-optic cable.

He references games, but this premise holds true anytime our kids are online. When parents embrace tech, we can start to understand it more fully and think about what each new technology introduces to our children. We need to be aware, educate ourselves, and introduce technology to our kids in a meaningful, thoughtful, and structured way.

I wrote this book to share what I'd learned about the inner workings of these types of platforms and apps, so that we can be better guides for our kids.

By engaging them in conversations about what we dis-

---

2   Jordan Shapiro, *The New Childhood* (New York: Little, Brown, 2018).

cover together, we can equip our children to grow up and thrive in this new tech-enhanced world.

CHAPTER ONE

THERE'S AN APP FOR THAT (INCLUDING VALIDATION)

How would your childhood have been different if you'd grown up in the age of social media?

I'll always remember an incident that happened in the fifth grade, when I was playing outside at recess. I was often picked on in elementary school because I was overweight, nerdy, and extremely naïve. I had a lot of allergies as a kid, and in particular I was allergic to dandelions. On this particular day, a group of bullies approached me on the playground, and without warning, they tackled me and pinned me down on the ground.

As I struggled to twist out of their grip, another kid pulled a fistful of dandelions out of the grass. He smashed them in my face and rubbed them over my neck and arms. I had a bad allergic reaction, and my skin broke out in an angry red rash. I had to go home that day—and I was terrified to go back to school the next day.

While that experience still sticks in my mind, it may not have stayed in the memories of those bullies. If the same incident were to happen today, though, you can bet that one of those kids would have been there with a device, taking a video. That awful experience would have been recorded, posted, and spread across the school—not just as a story, but as an experience that people could watch on permanent record. Even people who weren't there would have seen my struggle and my reaction.

While social media has made our interactions more accessible, instantaneous, and permanent, the drivers behind our behavior are still the same: we humans are driven by social validation.

I met my friend Jason in elementary school. I'm not sure if it was out of pity, but he was the one guy in the cool crowd who stood up for me. I followed Jason to high school—to a different school than the one my tormentors attended—and things started to turn around. Jason quickly got into the cool circles with the athletic types, and he brought me along. I had grown taller and thinned down, and I was starting to come into my own. I was actually a pretty decent athlete, and I joined the football and hockey teams. It was through those sports that I met Barney: he was charismatic, he was cool, and he was the ringleader of the athletic crowd.

Through these friendships, I became part of the inner circle. For the first time in my life, I was *in*, and I loved it. I even remember being invited to a kid's party—in elementary school I was rarely invited to parties—and at the party Barney turned to Jason and while pointing at me said, "Hey, so this is a pretty cool guy."

I didn't realize it at the time, but knowing what I know now, I'm sure my brain was flooding with dopamine in that moment.

It wasn't until later that I picked up on the peer pressure that comes with being part of a group. Some of the dumbest things I've ever done were driven by my need to fit in. One day in my senior year, a dozen or so of us football players were hanging out in the hallway at school. I did not want to lose my friends for anything, and so I said nothing as we made lines on either side of the hallway, waiting for new kids to pass. As unsuspecting ninth-graders approached us, we would pinball them down the line, shoving them back and forth across the hall.

I did nothing to stop us. Worse, I participated even though I'd been bullied myself and knew what it felt like. I wish I could have been as strong as Jason, who had stood up for me, especially because I knew what it was like to be on the other side of bullying. I've always been uncomfortable with that memory; especially as a father, I feel awful that I never stood up to my friends.

So why did I do it? Above anything else, I feared rejection from my friends.

UNDERSTANDING OUR NEED TO BELONG

Humans are wired to fit in with group dynamics and predict our place in the group, an idea made famous by Abraham Maslow. Most of us at some point in our education were introduced to Maslow's hierarchy of needs. Maslow studied human motivation, and in 1943, he introduced his eminent paper entitled "A Theory of Human Motivation." He believed that humans are motivated for personal growth and change through basic needs, organized into a five-stage model:

1. Biological and physiological needs including air, food, and shelter
2. Safety needs including protection, security, and law
3. Love and belonging needs
4. Esteem needs, such as recognition and respect from others
5. Self-actualization, or a desire to fully reach one's potential

Maslow argued that people move up the hierarchy in terms of basic motivation. Once we are fed, sheltered, safe, and secure, our motivation shifts to belongingness. He explained it this way:

> It is quite true that man lives by bread alone—when there is no bread. But what happens to man's desires when there is plenty of bread and when his belly is chronically filled?

At once other (and "higher") needs emerge and these, rather than physiological hungers, dominate the organism. And when these in turn are satisfied, again new (and still "higher") needs emerge and so on. This is what we mean by saying that the basic human needs are organized into a hierarchy of relative prepotency.[1]

Under this lens, it's easy to see why we feel so much comfort from fitting into cliques. On the other hand, we feel pain when we're left out. In elementary school, I often found myself on the outside looking in: I was almost always left out of birthday parties and other events with my peers. I felt intense pain from social exclusion in those early years.

Where I grew up in Saskatchewan, the elementary school system ranges from kindergarten to grade eight, and then you go to high school for grades 9 through 12. When I finally got to switch schools in high school, it was a new beginning. Through Jason, I became friends with many in the cool crowd, and suddenly, I was *in*. And I was willing to go along with the group to stay "in," even if that meant picking on the freshmen in the hallway.

We go to extremes to fit in. In a 1995 study of social belonging, researchers Roy F. Baumeister and Mark R. Leary found that "members of some groups are pressured

---

1   Saul McLeod, "Maslow's Hierarchy of Needs," *SimplyPsychology*, 2018.

to commit violent acts ranging from vandalism to murder in order to be accepted and demonstrate commitment to the group."[2]

The behavior I engaged in to seem cool to my buddies wasn't violent, but it was consistent with a larger phenomenon of human nature.

Baumeister and Leary illustrated this phenomenon further in their study "The Need to Belong," which remains one of the most cited studies on the subject. They looked at the work of dozens of researchers from Freud to Maslow and argued that the notion of belonging was often discussed but lacked conclusive empirical evidence. They set out to test their hypothesis: "Human beings have a pervasive drive to form and maintain at least a minimum quantity of lasting positivity and significant interpersonal relationships."

The need to belong, they proposed, has two main features:

> First, people need frequent personal contacts or interactions with the other person. Ideally, these interactions would be affectively positive or pleasant, but it is mainly important that the majority be free from conflict and neg-

---

2   Roy F. Baumeister and Mark R. Leary, "The Need to Belong: Desire for Interpersonal Attachments as a Fundamental Human Motivation," *Psychological Bulletin* 117, no. 3 (1995): 497–529.

ative affect. Second, people need to perceive that there is an interpersonal bond or relationship marked by stability, affective concern, and continuation into the foreseeable future.

Their work was predicated on the basis that the need to belong is driven by an "evolutionary basis" in which the need to belong in groups would have had benefits for our ancestors to survive and to reproduce.

They further argued that "if belonging is indeed a fundamental need, then aversive reactions to a loss of belongingness should go beyond negative affect to include some types of pathology."

Baumeister and Leary described the fundamental effect our need to belong has on our emotions. In the study, they stated, "Many of the strongest emotions people experience, both positive and negative, are linked to belongingness. Evidence suggests a general conclusion that being accepted, included, or welcomed leases to a variety of positive emotions, whereas becoming rejected, excluded or ignored leads to potent negative feelings (e.g., anxiety, depression, grief, jealousy and loneliness)."

An earlier study by Baumeister and Dianne M. Tice (1990) even went so far as to say that social exclusion could be the most significant cause of anxiety.[3] And as researchers continued to investigate the importance of belonging, a 2003 study of fMRI scans showed that being rejected activates the same parts of the brain as physical pain.[4]

This explains why particularly painful memories of rejection stick with us.

THE PROBLEM WITH BIRTHDAY CAKE

I can share with you a personal version of this from my unforgettable days as a sixth-grader. Similar to the bullies with dandelions incident, I'll always remember the birthday cake. I was very excited to be invited to a birthday party, and all the kids there were having a grand old time. As I've said, in grade school I was a hefty, overweight kid. I couldn't wait for the cake. When it was finally served up, I had more than one helping. I mean, I *really* enjoyed that cake; it was delicious. I had no idea it would come back to haunt me.

---

3   Roy F. Baumeister and Dianne M. Tice, "Anxiety and Social Exclusion," *Journal of Social and Clinical Psychology* 9, no. 2 (1990): 165–95.

4   N. I. Eisenberger, M. D. Lieberman, and K. D. Williams, "Does Rejection Hurt? An fMRI Study of Social Exclusion," *Science* 302, no. 5643 (2003): 290–92.

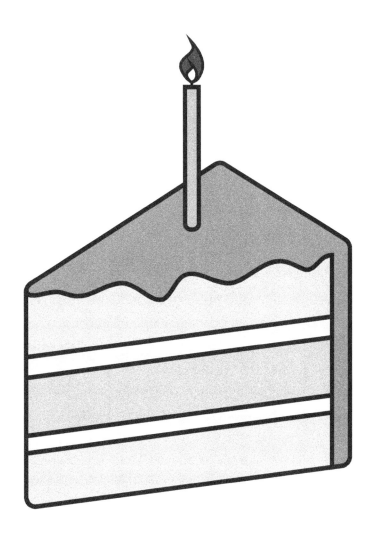

In math class a couple of days later, we had to come up with our own question and the teacher made us read them aloud. One of the students decided to be "funny" and said, "If I had a cake with ten slices and Sean came over and ate half of them, how many are left?" That really hurt.

I laughed along with the rest of the class, but I was trying to hold back tears.

Later in the same class, the teacher read another question featuring pigs to help us with division. "How many pigs would be in each group if we split twenty-four pigs into four equal groups?"

The same smart-alecky kid jumped in and said, "Don't you mean twenty-four *Seans*?" The class laughed like crazy. I tried to pretend I was laughing along, but by then I could feel the tears start to stream down my face.

Why do memories like this stick with us? Baumeister and Leary have the answer: the negative effects of rejection may very well outweigh the positive effects of inclusion. In "The Need to Belong," they concluded, "The need to belong can be considered a fundamental human motivation and the desire for interpersonal attachment may well be one of the most far-reaching and integrative constructs currently available to understand human nature."

FEELING INCLUDED IN THE AGE OF SMARTPHONES

Social validation isn't new, of course; humans craved it long before the emergence of smartphones. But we accessed it in different ways, such as sports and social activities. The rise of tech has drastically changed how we approach our sense of belonging by injecting instant feedback and convenience into our social interactions.

Facebook, Instagram, Snapchat, and the rest have introduced new mechanisms for social validation. We used to assess our social standing primarily by the quality of our face-to-face interactions. Today, we can tell someone we "like" them with a tap on a screen. Collecting "likes" and friends has become a scorecard to measure our social belonging, especially for kids growing up with these technologies. Our sense of acceptance has shifted from a primarily subjective feeling to objective vanity metrics we accrue on social media.

It's evident today that more kids are scratching their group dynamic itch through social media rather than sports or similar group activities. A study by the Aspen Institute published in the October 16, 2018, *Washington Post* shows the number of children aged 6 to 12 that regularly played a team sport fell to 37 percent in 2017 from 41.5 percent in 2011.[5] We can argue all day long on the cause of this decrease—be it that many sports are cost prohibitive or that screen time is replacing sports—but the fact is that lower participation in team sports and other group activities means more children must find belongingness in other ways. Many of them turn to social media.

---

5   Jacob Bogage, "Youth Sports Still Struggling with Dropping Participation, High Costs and Bad Coaches, Study Finds," *Washington Post,* October 16, 2018.

It can be hard to measure just how many young users are joining social media, because stats about social media users are only available for people 13 and up: the age restriction, technically, for those platforms. But as you might have guessed, many kids are getting on to those platforms before the age of 13—some of them *significantly* earlier. There are limited stats available for kids under 13, so most of what is presented throughout this book refers to teens, but we know younger and younger users are exposed to the same influences and behaviors.

NEW METRICS TO MEASURE OUR BELONGING

Knowing your place in the group was pretty straightforward "in the good old days." I remember feeling ecstatic when the phone rang, and I was invited to parties or to somebody's house to hang out and play video games or goof off around town. I waited by the phone plenty of weekday afternoons for a call from anybody; it made me feel like part of the group and I was terrified of being excluded from it.

If social media was around back then, I imagine what metrics I might have looked for to understand where I stood in the group. I would have expected to scroll through Jason's or Barney's social media posts and find that they were "liked" more than mine. But there might be someone else out there I considered equal to me in the social-standing scheme of things. Would I make a point to see how many "likes" that person's post got compared to mine, just to see where I stood in the group? I'm confident I would have.

Today's technology has formed a world where kids only have to tap into their go-to social media channels to see if they've been included or excluded. For example, if Jason included me in an event, I'd get to see and post photos of the experience. That's great, but what about kids connected to me, who weren't included by Jason? Through my social media feeds, they would see all the ways I was included in Jason's activities and parties—and they weren't. Because of our need to belong, if we're not part of the scene, we simply don't feel "worthy."

Think of how this scorecarding effect gets compounded

across the billions of users tapping into social media. A January 2018 study showed that on Instagram alone, there are 61 million users between the ages of 13 and 17, and an additional 246 million between the ages of 18 and 24. There are 500 million daily active users viewing, sharing, and liking 95 million photos and videos every day.[6] We have access to incredible amounts of data about what our friends like, who they're hanging out with, and whether we belong.

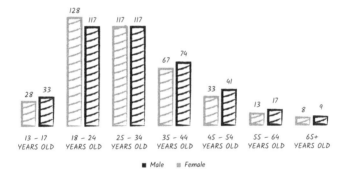

Profile of Instagram Users

Instagram Monthly Active Users,
by Age and Gender (in millions)

THE FOBLO IS REAL

Many children and young adults today post nearly everything they do through social media. While it looks and

---

6   Simon Kemp, "Digital in 2018: World's Internet Users Pass the 4 Billion Mark," *We Are Social*, January 30, 2018.

feels wonderful in the moment, social media's instant record makes interactions less resilient. Children are hyper-aware of exclusion, and the negative outcomes of *not* joining the crowd are incredibly powerful. Simply put, being rejected or excluded hurts more than the positive feelings of being included. It's great to be invited to the cool kid's party, but not being invited can be a crushing blow.

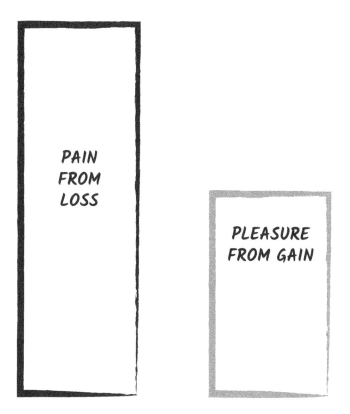

This bias is known as *loss aversion*: the notion that everything else being equal, a person would rather avoid losing than acquire an equivalent gain. Someone losing $100 gambling or in the stock market, for example, experiences a greater negative feeling than the positive feeling of winning $100. Consider the correlations this concept has for social media: a single post may earn dozens or even hundreds of "likes" for a day, but the thrill doesn't last. How does the same user feel about themselves the next day when their new post gets ignored?

Every social-media-savvy kid out there knows the term FOMO, the fear of missing out; and right along with it is FOBLO, the fear of being left out. These fears are so strong that we often do whatever it takes to avoid being excluded. But are we fully aware of how social media plays into our fears?

Sadly, there are a great number of documented cases of children battling social anxiety related to feelings of exclusion. I recently heard about a young girl named Lisa, who logged on to Instagram and saw posts from a surprise party for one of her friends. Twenty people showed up, and hundreds of photos were shown on the posts.

Lisa wasn't invited. She learned later it was just an oversight by the parent of the birthday girl, but in spite of this, Lisa was deeply hurt. She spoke about how she struggled with the emotional fallout of this rejection for a very long time.

While that scenario was unintentional, there are also stories of kids using social media to be intentionally malicious. I heard a story recently about a girl who attended a popular group's party. When she found a post from the party on social media, she tagged someone who wasn't there—someone she didn't like—to show they weren't included. "We're at this great party," she wrote. "Too bad you're not invited."

This is the negative side of instant gratification. The worst part is that these records of how we include and exclude others become permanent records in the digital age. In these examples, face-to-face interactions may have helped the girls sort things out. But on public posts in social networks, even innocent comments can affect our sense of belonging. These interactions get quickly circulated through social circles and schools and become a driving force in the online behavior of children and young adults. The records of these interactions become virtual dark clouds that don't ever really go away.

AVATARS GONE AWRY

Our sense of belonging also shapes how we present ourselves online. In *The New Childhood,* author Jordan Shapiro takes a critical look at avatars, the online personas we can create to accompany social media interactions.

Shapiro points out that avatars are very much alive in the ways that we craft, mold, and iterate on them.[7]

We then receive social validation of this online persona through comments, "likes," and other metrics which give us real-time feedback on our avatars. The desire to belong feeds our online personas; we create and mold our online selves based on this feedback from others. Over time, we can iterate in the direction that receives the most "likes" or positive reaction from people and move toward "our ideal self." But is it the real thing?

Many of us have different versions of ourselves. We bring out different facets of our personality at work, at school, or at home; I know I do. But social media introduces the ability to create a much more heavily curated version of ourselves, tailored with the artificial measuring stick of outside feedback. In the end, we may move into personas based on popularity rather who we really are.

HANDLE SOCIAL MEDIA WITH CARE

My memories of inclusion and exclusion had a lasting effect on me. Imagine what the same experiences would feel like today: each of those incidents probably would have been recorded, shared, posted on social media, and circulated throughout the school by the end of the day.

7   Jordan Shapiro, *The New Childhood* (New York: Little, Brown Spark, 2018).

Those posts might resurface years later to create the same negative impact they did in the original moment. The permanence of it all is a major driving force for children's behavior today.

What would your social life have looked like if you grew up in a digitally accessed world?

The number of young people connecting with social media is rapidly trending up. Parents must play an active role in ensuring that their children know how to use social networks responsibly. They need to help their children understand the outcomes of their online behavior, both for the impact their interactions have on other people and the effect social media has on their own mental health and sense of belonging.

It's not enough to let children loose to explore the online world alone. They need to be educated and mentored about what it means to be a good digital citizen today. Unfortunately, virtually all of today's top tech platforms aren't going to teach them—in fact, they are designed to enforce value in the wrong things, and above all else, to keep us screen captured. So, it will be up to us as parents to educate and be educated on the role of technology in our children's lives.

CHAPTER TWO

THIS IS YOUR BRAIN ON SOCIAL MEDIA

"How was your day today, honey?" My daughter was in the next room, twenty feet away. I could see her sitting in her favorite chair, looking at her tablet.

No reply. I tried again.

"What are you working on in there? Can you tell me about it?"

Still nothing.

When I looked closer I noticed a familiar sight: Kaylie's eyes were glossed over and she was statue still, staring at the screen. She was deep into something on YouTube, and didn't hear a word I said. I'm not sure she even knew I was in the house. Like a lot of parents, I started worrying: *Is this a sign of tech addiction? An attention disorder? Is this healthy?*

What is going on inside her brain?

I subsequently dove down a rabbit hole of research into the effect that technology is having on our brains. What I found—particularly about the effects of social media on our brain chemistry—shaped the features I would go on to develop in my own messenger for families, including kids. Just as importantly, my research shaped the features that wouldn't be included in our platform. And, of course, it shaped the conversations I've had with Kaylie since that day.

One of the best resources I had to learn more about this was Adam Alter's book *Irresistible: The Rise of Addictive Technology and the Business of Keeping Us Hooked* (a book I recommend for all parents).[1] Alter's work looks at behavioral addiction in the context of tech. He follows the chemical impact of dopamine as it floods the brain and triggers a corresponding reward cycle. Through individual stories, he illustrates the impact this cycle has on real people. One chilling example: he discusses online gamers who developed such an addiction to World of

---

1   Adam Alter, *Irresistible* (New York: Penguin, 2017).

Warcraft that they had to enroll in rehab treatment centers to recover.

Let's get this out of the way. The authoritative resource in the US on psychological diagnoses, the Diagnostic and Statistical Manual (DSM-V) published by the American Psychiatric Association, does not list "technology addiction" as a disorder. However, there's a healthy debate around the word "addiction" as it relates to tech use.[2] Several of the resources I cite refer to tech addiction, and I use the word at times. I have no intent to debate the word "addiction"—in the context of this book we may use words like "obsession," "infatuation," or "compulsion" with the same meaning. It is more important to view the larger picture as opposed to arguing over the use of the word.

Dopamine is a neurotransmitter that signals pleasure and reward to the brain, and it's a powerful driver of our behavior. Generally, it's a brain chemical that makes us feel good—but it can also turn dangerous when it becomes fuel for addictive behavior.

What if this chemical reaction in our brains could be used to exploit us, or to drive our behavior? Unfortunately, we can look to real-life examples of how dopamine is being

---

2   Anya Kamenetz, "Is 'Gaming Disorder' an Illness? WHO Says Yes, Adding It to Its List of Diseases," *NPR,* May 28, 2019.

used to game people in Las Vegas, and—as you'll see later on in this chapter—in Silicon Valley.

JACKPOT!

Of all the games in a casino, blackjack and poker give you some measure of control, and as an analytical guy and a CFA Charterholder, these are the gambles I occasionally play for fun. When you look at the probabilities at work on the gaming floor, the entire enterprise is designed for the casino to eventually win. This is especially true when it comes to the slots.

I've never really understood the appeal of slot machines. I've always thought of them as machines installed with a chip programmed to eventually take all your money. That chip, I later learned, is programmed for a much deeper goal. Long before social media, the gaming industry understood the dopamine reward loop and exploited it to lure people with the anticipation of what could be.

Most people know it doesn't make logical sense to gamble their money, because as the saying goes, the house always wins. The outcome will be negative more often than positive. But researchers have discovered that what drives us to gamble—and what makes it incredibly addicting—is not the natural high we get when we win; it's the *anticipation* of the reward.

DOPAMINE DEFINED

What exactly is dopamine? Discovered in 1957, dopamine is one of about twenty major neurotransmitters in our bodies. These neurotransmitters are the chemical messengers that keep our systems running smoothly: they coordinate our heartbeat and our breathing. They also transfer signals that initiate our behavior, and dopamine in particular regulates movement. It tells us to reach for a glass of water when we're thirsty, for example. Dopamine is a key factor in our motivation.[3]

Wolfram Schultz, professor of neuroscience at Cambridge University, looked closely at this process in a series of 1980s experiments on rats which showed that dopamine is related to reward received for an action, especially when that reward is anticipated. Schultz and his fellow researchers placed pieces of apple behind a screen and immediately saw a major dopamine response when the rat bit into the food.

Schultz discerned that dopamine was common to all mammals, and that it was the basis of learning: when a rat anticipated a bite of apple and the reward was met, it got a dopamine hit alongside the reward. The rat would then be motivated to repeat the behavior, and it could become a habit (or even an addiction). If the rat anticipated food

---

3   Simon Parkin, "Has Dopamine Got Us Hooked on Tech?" *The Guardian*, March 4, 2018.

but bit into something else, the rat learned very quickly what brought pleasure and what did not.

I understood the cause-and-effect basis of Schultz's research but wanted to know more: how do we get "hooked" on dopamine? I found answers through the work of Robert Sapolsky.

Sapolsky is an author and Stanford University professor of neurology and neurosurgery. In a presentation entitled, "Dopamine Jackpot! Sapolsky on the Science of Pleasure," he discusses a curious phenomenon he found in the dopamine cycle. Specifically, he looked at the sequence of events in the course of a task: first we receive a signal from our brains, then we perform the work, and we receive the reward. Dopamine is known as the "reward" chemical, so one might expect the dopamine levels to rise after receiving the reward.

But that's not what happens. Dopamine doesn't hit the brain *after* a reward; instead, it hits at the *signal*. In fact, the surge of dopamine mostly drops off by the time the reward is reached. Dopamine is the motivator that causes us to seek out a reward.

Sapolsky confirmed that dopamine is not about pleasure, but the *anticipation* of pleasure.[4] Dopamine, he said, is the chemical equivalent of the pursuit of happiness, rather than happiness itself.

Next, Sapolsky introduced a variable reward, and looked at the effect it had on dopamine. He set up a study to watch what happened to monkeys' dopamine responses as they pulled a lever to receive food. At first, he doled out food with every lever pull: the monkeys pulled the lever ten times and received food ten times. Then he introduced variability. On the next ten lever pulls, the monkeys only got food half the time.

And what happened to their dopamine? It shot through the roof.

Sapolsky saw varying levels of dopamine in response to how variable the reward was. Dopamine rose higher when monkeys received food 25 or 75 percent of the time than if they received food 100 percent of the time. But the highest dopamine hit came when there was 50 percent variability. Why? 50 percent brings with it the greatest level of uncertainty.

---

4   Robert Sapolky, "Dopamine Jackpot! Sapolsky on the Science of Pleasure" (presentation, California Academy of Sciences, San Francisco, CA, February 15, 2011).

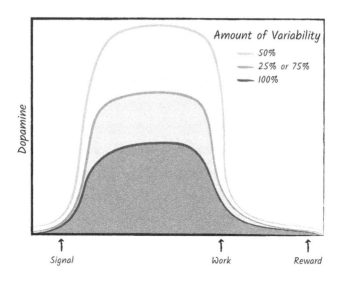

Sapolsky summed up the effect this way: "You've introduced the word 'maybe' into the equation. And 'maybe' is addictive like nothing else out there."

When it comes to gambling, Sapolsky's work reveals the linchpin: if dopamine release was tied only to reward, gambling would not be nearly so addictive. It's the anticipation of the reward—and especially the variability of when we receive it—that keeps us hooked. Without the thrill of anticipation, our logic would reign supreme and we'd know when the odds were stacked against us.

Slots are the epitome of variable reward. We pull the lever and watch the wheel spin and click into place one by one. Dopamine hits hardest when we think that next wheel might make us rich.

"WE'LL GET YOU EVENTUALLY"

Silicon Valley, it turns out, is not far behind in playing the game. You don't have to visit Vegas to pull the lever on your dopamine. Simply post on your platform of choice, and watch the "likes," shares, and comments roll in. Or, more distressingly, watch how they don't. Like the chip in a slot machine, many of Silicon Valley's brightest minds have programmed variable rewards into apps to hold your attention.

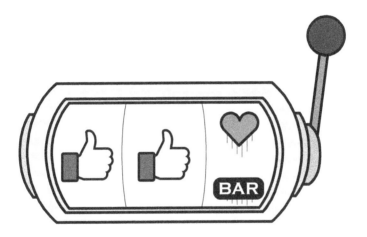

Facebook's founding president Sean Parker spoke to the widespread effect of social media in an interview during a 2017 Axios event in Philadelphia.

> When Facebook was getting going, people would come up to me and say, "I'm not on social media because I value real-life interactions. I value the moment and presence." I'd reply with a short declaration of, "Okay, but you know

you will be." People would often continue to deny it and I simply said, "We'll get you eventually"...I don't know if I really understood the consequences of what I was saying, because the unintended consequences of a network when it grows to a billion or two billion people...literally changes your relationship with society, with each other...it probably interferes with productivity in weird ways. God only knows what it's doing to our children's brains.[5]

But social media companies are very much aware of the way they manipulate the dopamine cycle to keep users engaged with their apps, and it's an issue that needs our attention. In the *New York Times* op-ed piece "How Evil Is Tech?" David Brooks remarked, "Tech companies understand what causes dopamine surges in the brain and they lace their products with 'hijacking techniques' that lure us in and create 'compulsion loops.'"[6]

Brooks' comment is corroborated by what Sean Parker went on to say in the *Axios* interview. "How do we consume as much of your time and conscious attention as possible?" Parker asked. His answer: "We need to sort of give you a little dopamine hit every once in a while, because someone 'liked' or commented on a photo or a post or whatever. And that's going to get you to contribute

---

5   Mike Allen, "Sean Parker Unloads on Facebook: 'God Only Knows What It's Doing to Our Children's Brains,'" *Axios*, November 9, 2017.

6   David Brooks, "How Evil Is Tech?" *New York Times,* November 20, 2017.

more content, and that's going to get you...more 'likes' and comments."

Parker described the gamification he and other social media moguls created by design on their apps. "It's a social-validation feedback loop...exactly the kind of thing that a hacker like myself would come up with, because you're exploiting a vulnerability in human psychology." Chillingly, he described how "the inventors, creators—it's me, it's Mark [Zuckerberg], it's Kevin Systrom on Instagram, it's all of these people—understood this consciously. And we did it anyway."

Not only are the world's biggest social media empires aware of the effects of dopamine and variable reward, but they are ardently using it to their advantage.

JUST ONE MORE HIT

Remember, dopamine comes to us in short bursts. You anticipate something, get a hit of dopamine, and then dopamine levels drop. Addiction takes hold by trying to take that feeling to higher levels over time. You can see this in action by watching people at a casino; they mindlessly keep pulling the lever to get the next hit, and the next hit after that. Humans are wired to want more, to anticipate more, to get a greater reward; and that's where addiction comes in.

In the context of social media, clicking "post" is very much like pulling the lever on the slot machine, because there's a variable reward in the form of "likes" or comments or shares of your post. That's why we keep posting even if we're not getting the reward we want; with a variety in the response comes increased anticipation.

We get more of a dopamine rush without consistent validation from others; we wait in anticipation of posts paying off. Consider another gambling example: In blackjack, the anticipation of the cards being dealt triggers the biggest dopamine hit. That second card might be a winner or a bummer, but the anticipation keeps people glued to the game. Posting on social media is like the dealing of the cards; you just don't know what the outcome will be.

Why do we care so much about "likes" and what people say about our posts and how many of them chime in? Because we're inherently driven by our need to belong, as we discussed in the last chapter, and social validation is driven by a chemical process in our brains that feeds on reward. If we get 100 "likes" on a post, we innately want 120 or 150 next time. We compare the popularity of our past posts or our peers' content to predict what our next post will bring, and want a bigger and better hit. In this case, the addiction is social validation using engagement, or vanity metrics, to gauge where we think we are.

Let's say my posts are getting twenty-five "likes" and a friend of mine sees 250. I'm naturally wired to turn my twenty-five into fifty into 100 because my perception of my social standing improves. This idea of climbing the social ladder through media is very important to young people today in the relentless charge to be "liked" by everyone.

This is what I saw in my daughter's behavior with PopJam, and what drove my concern. Similarly, Kaylie seems particularly interested in how other peoples' posts performed: my wife and I don't post much on Instagram or other platforms, but when we do, my daughter is always curious how many "likes" we've gotten. But now, knowing what that anticipation means for her brain, I recognize there's a bigger issue behind her curiosity. When she asks, I remind Kaylie that counting "likes" isn't what is important, but might point out that Uncle Tony or Uncle Adam have "liked" a family photo as a way to say hi to us.

As our children explore the online world, it's important to educate them on what behaviors social media companies are deliberately trying to steer us toward.

You don't have to take my word for it: several of the original puppet masters of social media are beginning to acknowledge their responsibility in shaping our online lives. Many of the original designers of these features are now speaking out against the obsessive behavior their designs have promoted.

BRAIN HACKING

"I feel tremendous guilt," Chamath Palihapitiya admitted to an audience of Stanford students during an interview at the Graduate School of Business. Palihapitiya was a former Vice President of User Growth at Facebook, and when asked about his involvement in exploiting consumer behavior, he replied, "The short-term, dopamine-driven feedback loops that we have created are destroying how society works."[7]

He's not the only one with feelings of remorse, or at least recognition of what is happening. After years of premeditated scheming and untold millions invested in driving user engagement, key players in social media are starting to change their tune. Tristan Harris, former product manager and design ethicist at Google, is one of the most active advocates against obsessive behavior in social media, and he's forcing change at some of the largest organizations in social media.

While at Google, Harris warned technology companies about the "arms race to capture attention" and the need

---

7   Trevor Haynes, "Dopamine, Smartphones & You: A Battle for Your Time," *Harvard University* (blog), May 1, 2018.

for responsible design. Harris left Google in 2016 and launched a nonprofit initiative called Time Well Spent, aimed at encouraging tech companies to adopt better design practices. Since then, Google and Apple have added "time well spent" features to iOS and Android phones.[8]

In 2018, Harris launched the Center for Humane Technology. I urge all parents to familiarize themselves with Tristan Harris' work, which speaks to many of the issues presented in this book.

In a very popular 2017 segment of *60 Minutes*, Anderson Cooper talked with Harris on brain hacking, featuring Snapchat as a vivid example.

In the interview, Harris reminds us that Snapchat is currently the most popular messaging service for teenagers and the platform now includes Snapstreaks, which shows the number of days in a row that you've traded messages with someone—a feature that plays heavily into the hands of the dopamine hit as users attempt to keep their streaks going.

Doesn't seem like that big a deal, right? On the surface, maybe not, but Harris explained a surprising result of teens' infatuation with the streak.

8   "About Tristan Harris," *TristanHarris.com*, 2019.

Kids don't want to lose their streak, to the point that when they go on vacation are so stressed about their streak that they actually give their password to five other kids to keep their streaks going on their behalf. And so you could ask, when these features are being designed, are they designed to most help people live their life? Or are they being designed because they're best at hooking people into using the product?[9]

His conversation highlights the fact that validation metrics matter—and they matter a lot. Harris pointed out that some people say it's just the modern-day equivalent of gossiping on the phone "back in the day," but technology has made this new phenomenon distinctly different.

The problem, he says, is that "your telephone in the 1970s didn't have a thousand engineers on the other side of it who were redesigning it to work with other phones and then updating the way your phone worked every day in order to be more and more persuasive."

The same is true for television. Like most every other kid in pre-smartphone days, I sat in front of the TV for hours. But as Jaron Lanier, computer scientist and outspoken

---

9   Anderson Cooper, "What Is 'Brain Hacking'? Tech Insiders on Why You Should Care," *60 Minutes*, April 9, 2017.

critic of social media, said: "When you watch the television, the television isn't watching you."[10]

On the same *60 Minutes* segment, Anderson Cooper spoke with Ramsay Brown, co-founder of the appropriately named Dopamine Labs. Brown first studied neuroscience before getting into tech. He described how apps look at user engagement, such as "likes" on an app, as "virtual currency," and they "spend" it in strategic ways to influence user behavior.

"They're holding some of your 'likes' back," Brown observed, "and then [they] deliver them later in a big burst. 'Here are thirty 'likes' from a little while ago.' But why that moment? It's simple: there's some algorithm somewhere that predicted that for this user right now who is experimental subject 79B3 in experiment 231, we think we can see an improvement in his behavior if you give it to him in this burst instead of that burst."

Think about that for a moment: some of the platforms you use every day are purposefully withholding "likes" on your content and delivering them to you at a time when it is most likely you'll take action. The objective, always, is to drive you back into the platform and get you to engage.

---

10   "Jaron Lanier Interview on How Social Media Ruins Your Life," YouTube video, posted by *Channel 4 News*, June 15, 2018.

Social media platforms are constantly gathering data about what stimulus will keep you online, and consciously using that knowledge to develop programs to keep you hooked. Algorithms tailor everything, from notifications to bursts of "likes," to motivate your behavior.

Kind of makes you feel like a rat or a monkey in a giant experiment, doesn't it?

ARE THE TIMES A-CHANGING?

If there is a silver lining in all this, it's that awareness is increasing. Consumers are beginning to move away from addictive features on their own, and more platforms are adapting to put less focus on manipulative features such as "likes" and streaks. In the following chapter, we'll take a look at two major changes Instagram has made in response to user behavior. But can we expect the platforms to lead the charge?

No way.

None of these platforms are making changes on their own; they're updating their features to adapt to changing tastes and declines in user-generated content. Users are driving the change. But as user tastes change, platforms are working quickly to understand the new behaviors and adapt their platforms to keep them "sticky."

As an example, recent news has drawn attention to the Facebook Research data app, a tool that is used internally at Facebook to track every action that users take on their phones. Algorithms can then crunch the data about user behavior to figure out how to get users to spend more time on Facebook.[11]

With the Facebook Research app, Facebook took advantage of an enterprise program in which Apple allows app developers to gather data from their employees. But Facebook later deployed the app to the public, which violated Apple's privacy guidelines. In addition, data was collected from kids as young as 13. Though the parents of those teens signed release forms, it raised questions about the ethics of collecting such a large amount of data from teens.

As the public learned about Facebook's extensive data gathering in early 2019, groups of people called on Apple's CEO Tim Cook to remove Facebook and its apps from Apple's App Store. Yet despite having its reputation dragged through the gutter in the wake of the research app and the Cambridge Analytica scandal (more on that later), Facebook continues to grow in revenue, profit, and users, the three metrics that drive the company's value. Like other social media giants, they clearly have no incen-

---

11   Kurt Wagner, "Apple Says It's Banning Facebook's Research App That Collects Users' Personal Information," *Vox*, January 30, 2019.

tive to stop what they are doing—they are continuing to grow amid these, and many other, controversies.

Though key tech company players have claimed remorse, these are the same people who learned about the dopamine effect and still decided to exploit it through their platforms. And many of them became extremely wealthy because of it. The ultimate goal for tech companies is still to drive users to their products. How they do that might look different in the near future, but they will still use the tools available to them to increase user engagement.

As the common refrain goes, the numbers don't lie. Platforms are driven by numbers of users and what they respond to, so advertisers can then put tailored ads in front of them at strategic times for the highest probability of user action. Consider this fact: every month, 4.7 billion people actively engage with YouTube, Facebook, Instagram, or Snapchat (though many are the same users on multiple platforms).[12] That's more than half the world. Even divided four ways, it's more than a billion users each.

---

12   Simon Kemp, "Digital in 2018: World's Internet Users Pass the 4 Billion Mark," *We Are Social*, January 30, 2018.

Active Users of Key Global Social Platforms

Monthly Active Users by Platform (in millions)

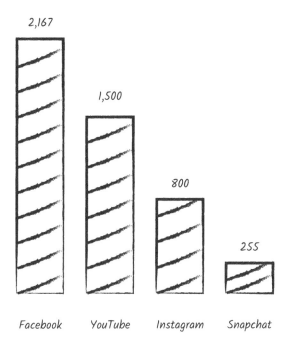

It's clear that social media is securely entrenched in modern society and our psyche, and it may be exacting a toll on our mental health.

SOCIAL MEDIA AND MENTAL HEALTH

Social ties have been linked to mental health since long

before the rise of social media.[13] As we saw in chapter 1, we have an inherent need to belong. Being part of the group is good for the psyche. Dr. Renae Beaumont, child psychologist, agrees. "Belongingness and feeling connected to others is a basic human need," she wrote when I asked her about how social media has impacted our sense of belonging. "Social media provides a platform to help achieve this sense of belonging, provided that it is used in a healthy way, and not at the expense of meaningful face-to-face relationship time."[14]

Using tech in healthy ways, Dr. Beaumont says, is difficult, particularly for tweens and teens:

> A lot of young people I work with, both boys and girls, compare themselves to online influencers and peers on platforms such as Instagram and feel that they do not measure up with regards to how they look, what they achieve, their popularity or their lifestyle. Having 24/7 online access to photo, video and text posts can fuel these downward social comparisons at an unprecedented level for those most vulnerable to making them. It often becomes a vicious cycle: those at greatest risk for low self-esteem, depression and social exclusion or rejection are at greatest risk of looking at online posts and comparing themselves

---

13   Ichiro Kawachi and Lisa F. Berkman, "Social Ties and Mental Health," *Journal of Urban Health* 78, no. 3 (2001).

14   Dr. Renae Beaumont, personal email communication with the author, March 17, 2019.

to others, which further fuels their low self-esteem, low mood and feelings of being a social misfit.

Smartphones and social media have given young users the tools to check up on their status and how they compare to others anytime, anywhere, and this ability may be hurting their mental health.

In her 2017 book *iGen*, author Jean Twenge, PhD, strongly correlates the use of smartphones and social media to what she describes as "skyrocketing" rates of teen depression and suicide.[15]

Twenge defines "iGen" as the generation of now-teens, born between 1995 and 2012, whose childhoods have been shaped by smartphones and social media. In an article in *The Atlantic*, Twenge goes as far as to say, "It's not an exaggeration to describe iGen as being on the brink of the worst mental-health crisis in decades."[16]

Twenge points to a 2016 National Survey on Drug Use and Health that looked at occurrences of major depressive episodes (MDEs). The study defined an MDE as a period of "two weeks or longer in the past year when they experienced a depressed mood or loss of interest or pleasure in daily activities, and they had at least some

15   Jean M. Twenge, *iGen* (New York: Simon and Schuster), 2017.

16   Jean M. Twenge, "Have Smartphones Destroyed a Generation?" *The Atlantic*, September 2017.

additional symptoms, such as problems with sleep, eating, energy, concentration, and self-worth." The study also delineated a second category, MDE with severe impairment, in which "their depression caused severe problems with their ability to do chores at home, do well at work or school, get along with their family, or have a social life."

The survey's findings revealed that 12.8 percent of adolescents aged 12 to 17 (3.1 million adolescents) had an MDE during the past year, and 9.0 percent of adolescents (2.2 million adolescents) had an MDE with severe impairment. And while that represented a spike from previous years among adolescents, it stayed flat for older age groups.

In *iGen*, Twenge also referenced an American College Health Association survey that showed the number of undergraduate students who seriously considered suicide or who intentionally injured themselves had increased dramatically from 2011 to 2016.

Twenge correlates these findings with the rise of smartphone use and social media engagement. While these studies offer evidence that depression may be on the rise among youth, I believe it is simply too early to declare tech as a singular, or even leading, cause.

There are inherent challenges in linking smartphone use

to mental health. In Twenge's book, published in 2017, she noted suicide rates were on the rise. However, to back her claim she used data up until 2015, when rates were actually lower than they were in the late 1980s and early 1990s, well before the onslaught of smartphones.[17] However, suicide rates have continued to rise in 2016 and 2017, and they're currently at the highest level of the past few decades. I agree that when looking at those numbers, where there's smoke there's probably fire, but correlation doesn't necessarily mean causation.

As a former financial analyst, I tend to look at data with a lot of scrutiny. I'm very interested in looking at methodology and statistical output and am very much aware of the concept of "spurious correlation." This happens when researchers draw connections between two variables that appear to be associated, but may not be in actuality. One of the most well-known examples is the "relationship" between the S&P return and the winner of the Super Bowl: for a while, when the AFC team won, the S&P was negative the following year, and when the NFC team won, the S&P return was positive the next year. The winning team could "predict" the S&P return with upwards of 90 percent accuracy. Over time, as you might expect, the effect has normalized and weakened the correlation between these two factors.

17   "Suicide Injury Deaths and Rates Per 100,000," accessed from "Injury Prevention & Control," *Centers for Disease Control and Prevention,* 2019.

Obviously these two variables are not connected, but we may be drawn to think so when we're looking for a pattern. Another classic example: each summer, crime rates increase. So do ice cream sales. Does more ice cream consumption lead to people committing crimes? It is more likely that crime rates go up in the summer for different reasons: because there are more people out in the streets, and people tend to be on vacation more, leaving their homes vacant. The factor that links rising ice cream sales and rising crime rates could be the rise in temperature. So a common factor can link these two variables, but it doesn't mean that each of these variables causes the other.

Similarly, the rise of both smartphone/social media use and rates of depression may not be directly correlated, but they may in fact be linked with other variables likely at play. Often, information about mental health is self-reported, which can carry a great deal of bias: the stigma associated with mental health is changing (perhaps, ironically, due to the willingness of people to share openly on social media), and that may be leading to more people self-declaring their mental health status.

There are also studies that present findings that contradict Twenge's assertions, though those studies are less than definitive in their conclusions (again, sample sizes aren't huge, and much of the data relies on self-reported feelings).

In a longitudinal study by Amy Orben, Tobias Dienlin, and Andrew K. Przybylski from the University of Oxford in the UK, the researchers concluded that "social media use is not, in and of itself, a strong predictor of life satisfaction across the adolescent population. Instead, social media effects are nuanced, small at best, reciprocal over time, gender specific, and contingent on analytic methods."[18]

In fact, Orben said in a *Guardian* article, "Changes in an adolescent's media use can explain only 0.25 percent of changes in their life satisfaction one year later. Vice versa, fluctuations in their life satisfaction can only explain 0.04 percent of changes in their social media use one year later, which is a tiny effect as well."[19]

In a more direct response to Twenge, another longitudinal study looked at two groups, adolescents and undergraduate students, for associations between social media use and depressive symptoms. The study concluded, "Results indicate that among both samples, social-media use did not predict depressive symptoms over time for males or females. However, greater depres-

18   Amy Orben, Tobias Dienlin, and Andrew K. Przybylski, "Social Media's Enduring Effect on Adolescent Life Satisfaction," *Proceedings of the National Academy of Sciences,* May 2019.

19   Nicola Davis, "Children's Social Media Use Has 'Trivial' Effect on Happiness—Study," *The Guardian,* May 6, 2019.

sive symptoms predicted more frequent social-media use only among adolescent girls."[20]

So we have representation from the extreme ends of the spectrum: on one side, social media has us on the brink of a mental health crisis, and on the other, it has a minuscule effect on mental health (less than 1 percent). Where is the truth? I don't think we know definitively just yet—I'm guessing that it lies somewhere in the middle. Intuitively, it seems like some of the things we see and read on social media simply can't be good for the psyche—again, where there's smoke there's likely some fire—but I'm not sure that it is a raging inferno either.

Social Media Effects on Mental Health

Much of the negative narrative about smartphone use hits home because it lines up with what many of us parents are currently observing in interactions with teens and younger kids. Recently, I saw a group of four teenagers sitting at a restaurant table. None of them were talking

20   Taylor Heffer, et al., "The Longitudinal Association between Social-Media Use and Depressive Symptoms among Adolescents and Young Adults," *Clinical Psychological Science*, January 29, 2019.

to each other; they all stared at their phones, and I didn't see a single smile. Any sort of meaningful connection between them was totally absent.

It is both alarming and common to see interactions like this, where people sitting three feet away from one another can seem so distant. I wondered whether the interaction (or lack thereof) I witnessed at the restaurant had a lasting impact on those teens.

What happens to our mental health when we turn away from in-person interactions and toward the networks on our phones?

DOES USING FACEBOOK MAKE YOU FEEL BAD?

Researchers Holly B. Shakya and Nicholas A. Christakis have been investigating this question and published their findings in the *American Journal of Epidemiology*[21] and *Harvard Business Review*.[22] Their conclusion: "Although real-world social networks were positively associated with overall well-being, the use of Facebook was negatively associated with overall well-being."

---

21 Holly B. Shakya and Nicholas A. Christakis, "Association of Facebook Use with Compromised Well-Being: A Longitudinal Study," *American Journal of Epidemiology*, May 9, 2016.

22 Holly B. Shakya and Nicholas A. Christakis, "A New, More Rigorous Study Confirms: The More You Use Facebook, the Worse You Feel," *Harvard Business Review*, April 10, 2017.

So, people who spend more time on social media networks report lower levels of well-being. This leads to another, bigger question that the study couldn't answer: did people's well-being suffer because they were on Facebook, or did people spend more time on Facebook because their well-being was suffering?

Shakya and Christakis point to the challenges of studying this topic and note that "more rigorous research is needed to untangle the relationship between social media use and well-being."

First among the challenges was that in the longitudinal study, they relied on people to self-report their mental health, and they didn't assess whether participants suffered from depression or other mental health conditions going in.

The second challenge in the study was the availability of Facebook data. A relatively small proportion of survey respondents gave permission for researchers to look at their Facebook data, and this reduction in sample size made it more difficult to identify conclusive associations.

Lastly, they weren't able to determine what activities on Facebook lead to a reduced sense of well-being. When users "liked" other people's positive posts, did that lead to a negative self-comparison? The researchers couldn't tell. Assessing this behavior alongside users' overall activity suggested "the relationships we found are simply a matter of quantity of use." Still, they reported that liking content, clicking links posted by friends, and updating one's status were all related to lower reported mental health, physical health, and life satisfaction.

Despite these limitations, researchers in this study were able to compare several different data metrics and found consistent results across each outcome: they agree that Facebook use does not promote well-being. They concluded that individual social media users might do well to curtail their use and instead focus on real-world relationships.

To me, the most surprising and interesting aspect of all this (and why I included it) is that even actions we consider to be positive—liking other people's posts and engaging with them—were negatively correlated with mental health in this particular study.

Are these activities, which seem positive on the surface, truly positive? It's possible that even positive posts and interactions create a negative effect when young people use them to compare themselves to their peers. There is probably a reason to be concerned—especially when we see youth measuring themselves in vanity metrics such as "likes" and reactions to their posts. In the next chapter, we'll see very real stories of the impact these metrics are having on young people.

CHAPTER THREE

WHAT'S NOT TO LIKE ABOUT A "LIKE"?

I first met Facebook in 2006, and it was love at first click. Like most everyone else, I reconnected with high school friends, shared events from my life, and stayed in tune with "all the latest." As time passed, however, interactions on the app seemed to get more disingenuous. People seemed less concerned with the quality of their interactions and more concerned with the quantity of friends they accumulated. My honeymoon phase with Facebook was over.

Things came to a head on my thirtieth birthday. I went to my Facebook wall and it was full of "Happy Birthday" posts. Facebook's algorithm automatically flashes notifications like birthdays to anyone connected to its users, directly or otherwise. Anyone even remotely connected to me saw the message, "It's Sean Herman's birthday today. Click here to wish him a Happy Birthday."

And they did. I had "Happy Birthday, Sean" posts all over the place, and a good many of them were from people I didn't even know. I don't want to sound harsh—I appreciated all the well wishes—but it all seemed so artificial.

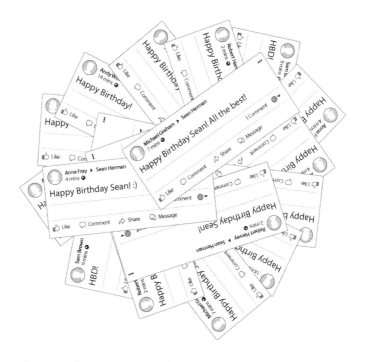

The next day I had some friends over for a barbecue and it hit me: I looked around and thought, *Most of the people who really matter to me are right here, physically in my house.* None of them were prompted by a machine to wish me a happy birthday; we were all together in a genuine way, and it was absolutely wonderful.

After my party, I removed my birth date from public on Facebook, and eventually deactivated my account altogether a few years later. (I did end up reactivating it many years later, but I don't use it in the same way I did back then.) When the quality of interactions with Facebook deteriorated for me, I completely lost interest.

Humans can only manage a finite social circle before losing the quality of connection we came for. In the 1990s, a British anthropologist, Robin Dunbar, even put a number on it. He proposed that humans can maintain only 150 stable relationships—this has become known as "Dunbar's number." Our social media use often stretches our networks beyond 150 friends, and those constant wide-ranging interactions can weaken our connections.

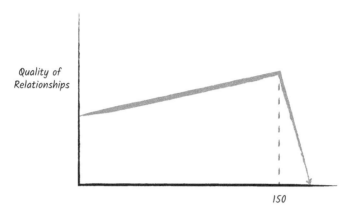

Dunbar's Number

Quality of Relationships

# of Relationships

150

TAKE YOUR THUMBS OFF THE DEVICE, AND SLOWLY BACK AWAY

At age 15, Australian-bred Essena O'Neill was a social media demigod. She was all over the big-name platforms and wildly popular on Instagram, with more than 500,000 followers. She scored modeling contracts, traveled the world, and made a ton of money.

"I grew up being a teen idol and social media famous at 15," O'Neill said in a letter she sent to fans upon leaving Instagram.[1] "At 12 I saw myself as this huge, too tall, nerdy, awkward, majorly unpopular girl. I thought to be social

---

[1] Essena O'Neill, newsletter to fans, 2016.

media famous would be the best job ever and if all these people 'liked' me, I would be happy."

O'Neill spent eight hours a day photographing, styling, editing, and filming for her social media posts. Her entire world revolved around social media, and from the outside it looked like the perfect life. At one point, though, she recognized the irony of becoming more popular every day but being "lonely and miserable inside." She had pushed away her "real" friends and only spent time with other people on social media.

"I smiled and laughed in pictures and vlogs but no one knew I had what is now described as social anxiety disorder, depression, and I was body dysmorphic. Whenever I met someone I instantly thought 'they hate me' or 'they make fun of my videos' or 'they think I'm stupid.' I was exhausted trying to keep up this bubbly, funny, happy facade."

Eventually, she walked away. She came to the realization, "Social media isn't real. It's purely contrived images and edited clips ranked against each other. I realized how I am never present and I don't really talk to people; and more so how my days had morphed into constant shoots, constant planning to do things to make my life look good on a screen."

One example is a popular photo of her in a bikini on a

beach. Everything in the shot looks perfect—but she later confided it took more than 100 attempts before she had her abs and the pose looking just the way she wanted. She began to speak to the phoniness of these highly produced posts and referred to Instagram as "a 2D version of yourself." O'Neill came to a realization that she was spending her entire life curating content for Instagram, and she found that she was actually quite unhappy.

The day before her nineteenth birthday, she posted an "unfiltered" video describing her desperation and her decision to quit social media. "I was scared," she wrote in her newsletter to fans. "I was throwing away such a big part of my life." She didn't review the video after creating it; she uploaded it, in its raw state, to YouTube.

The next morning, the stats were incredible: she'd had over a million views in 12 hours, and her Instagram following had jumped from 500,000 to 800,000. She saw the numbers on the screen and blinked in amazement.

And then, O'Neill shut down her accounts—Instagram, Facebook, Tumblr, Snapchat, YouTube, all of them.

What happened next shocked her: many of her followers turned on her. They posted mean, hateful comments. They called her decision a hoax and a publicity stunt. She later said she never thought, after being "Insta-famous," that all those people would turn around and publicly hate her.

It's a sad ending to her story—and I truly hope she is now living a much happier and fulfilled life and in the grand scheme—but her experience shed some light on a concerning issue.

IT'S NOT ALL ABOUT VANITY

All said and done, vanity metrics such as "likes," followers, post comments, retweets, and shares are marketing tools that introduce variable reward through social comparison. The addictive quality of social media has made it possible for people to brand themselves and bring in substantial income from sponsored posts.

Social media celebrities and influencers have accumulated legions of followers and then monetized the attention. Popular feeds—from teen models to mom bloggers—can make $20,000 per post and much higher. Famous feeds pull astounding numbers: Kylie Jenner earns $1M per post. Selena Gomez brings in $800,000.[2]

---

2   "Instagram Rich List 2018," *Hopper,* 2018.

Top 10 Social Media Rich List

RANK	NAME	FOLLOWERS	COST PER POST
1	Kylie Jenner	110,000,000	$1,000,000
2	Selena Gomez	138,000,000	$800,000
3	Christiano Ronaldo	133,000,000	$750,000
4	Kim Kardashian	113,000,000	$720,000
5	Beyonce Knowles	115,000,000	$700,000
6	Dwayne Johnson	109,000,000	$650,000
7	Justin Bieber	100,000,000	$630,000
8	Neymar da Silva Santos Junior	101,000,000	$600,000
9	Lionel Messi	95,300,000	$500,000
10	Kendall Jenner	92,400,000	$500,000

"Likes," then, don't just represent social currency, but real currency as well. The possibility of having a following turn into a salary adds an incentive to pile up numbers of followers, "likes," and comments.

One mobile design expert, Rameet Chawla, decided to capitalize on the impulse to accrue social wealth—and discovered a hack for accruing monetary wealth as well.

I came across Chawla's name in an article on *The Cut* titled, "Addicted to Likes: How Social Media Feeds Our Neediness."[3] His name sounded familiar to me, and a quick search reminded me that he was featured in Adam Alter's *Irresistible*.

In 2014, Chawla built an app called Lovematically, which

---

3   Maureen O'Connor, "Addicted to Likes: How Social Media Feeds Our Neediness," *New York*, February 20, 2014.

automatically "liked" everything that came across his Instagram post. "If all my Instagram friends feel great when they get 'likes,'" he said, "why not make them happy in an automated way that's easier for me too?"

In a post describing Lovematically on his company website, Fueled, Chawla explained the inspiration behind the program. He compared "likes" to crack cocaine, saying, "They've inconspicuously emerged as the first digital drug to dominate our culture."[4]

As the Lovematically bot "liked" all the incoming posts on his feed, Chawla quickly realized he had something big on his hands. The program was so efficient that within three months of running it on his own feed, he gained more than 2,700 followers.

He decided to release it into the world. It lasted only a few hours on Instagram before the platform got wise and shut it down (it violated Instagram's Terms of Service). Even so, Chawla went on to earn more than $500,000 in new development business from brands that recognized him from his exploitation of an Instagram loophole.[5]

Chawla's story embodies the dark side of social media's

---

4   Rameet Chawla, "Lovematically," *Fueled*, accessed April 17, 2019.

5   Erin Griffith, "How One Founder Used Instagram Likes to Earn $500K in Business," *Fortune*, February 14, 2014.

addictive tendencies. The social currency of "likes" has become so disingenuous that it could literally be disembodied—in the form of the Lovematically bot—to cash in on the dopamine cycle.

THE VALUE OF VANITY CURRENCY

In the *Washington Post* article "13, Right Now: This Is What It's Like to Grow Up in the Age of Likes, Lols and Longing," the author followed the social media lifestyle of an everyday 13-year-old girl.[6]

"Over 100 likes is good, for me. And comments. You just comment to make a joke or tag someone," she said. "The best thing is the little notification box, and happy birthday posts are a pretty big deal. It really shows who cares enough to put you on their page."

She has 604 followers, but only 25 photos on her page because she deletes most of what she posts—in fact, she cuts anything that doesn't get enough "likes."

She described an instance when she changed her Snapchat username, and was shocked to see her high score revert to zero. The Snapchat score tallies every post a user sends and receives. It was so "embarrassing and stressful"

---

6   Jessica Contrera, "13, Right Now: What It's Like to Grow Up in the Age of Likes, Lols and Longing," *Washington Post*, May 25, 2016.

to have a score of zero that she sent enough snaps to rack up a thousand points—in one day.

The defining lesson here: social media attention matters. "Likes" and points are a virtual currency that puts teens in their place of social standing. I've spoken to many young social media users, and the vast majority of teens admitted that they do count these things, or at least they're very much aware of them.

"Likes" matter so much, in fact, that millions of teens simply delete social media posts that don't receive enough "likes." In fact, the *Wall Street Journal* confirms more than half of Instagram users were in the habit of deleting "inadequate" posts.[7] This is a major issue for the platform, and it had to adjust.

UNDER PRESSURE

Social media platforms need us as users to continually post new content. Without user-generated content from our friends and those we follow, platforms would get stale quickly. Recent trends resulting in declining user-generated content have forced social media companies to adapt their features to keep users posting—especially young users, who have a lifetime of social media use

---

7   Deepa Seetharaman, "Instagram Unveils Instagram Stories," *Wall Street Journal*, August 2, 2016.

ahead of them. At the heart of these changes is the shifting relationship that youth is having with their "likes."

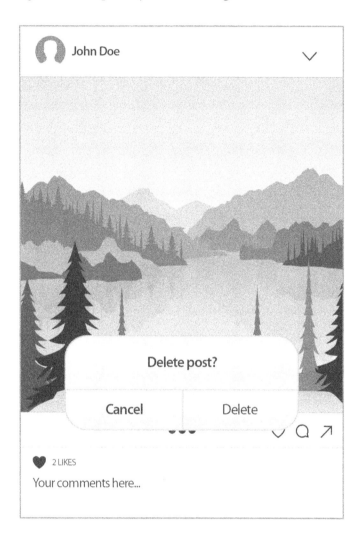

If you need more evidence that "likes" cause anxiety and performance pressure, look no further than two changes

Instagram has made to their platform in recent years in order to boost participation from users. With platforms of this size, changes like these are extremely significant (and costly)—as the old saying goes, it is hard to steer a large ship. So, I'd argue that even more than the studies cited earlier, these changes prove that "likes" come with pressure and anxiety, and are affecting our children (and the platforms).

EPHEMERAL STORIES

The first feature Instagram added in response to changing user behavior was "Stories." This addition allowed users to post personal feeds that would disappear automatically after twenty-four hours, a feature that closely resembled the immensely popular function of a competitive product, Snapchat. As an article in *Fortune* pointed out, Snapchat rode the wave of this immensely innovative and popular feature to the tune of 150 million daily active users by mid-2016. This also confirmed that users don't necessarily want to be judged every time they post a photo, and Instagram took notice.[8] As with Snapchat, there is no "liking" or similar commenting involved in Instagram's "Stories" feature.

---

8   Matthew Ingram, "Here's Why Facebook Is So Desperate to Buy, Copy or Kill Snapchat," *Fortune*, August 2, 2016.

Number of Snapchat
Daily Active Users (in millions)

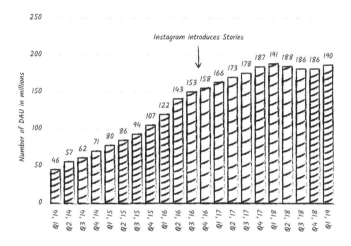

I viewed Instagram's introduction of "Stories" in 2016 as a purely competitive play at first—an answer to Snapchat's success at the time. Looking closer, however, I saw it was a response to a disturbing trend for the platform. Instagram users (especially young ones) were deleting a significant amount of their photos, because they weren't receiving enough "likes." Instagram's founder admitted as much after the introduction of the "Stories" feature.

In a *Wall Street Journal* article, Instagram's CEO Kevin Systrom spoke to the value behind the "Stories" feature. "We need to have a place where you feel free to post whatever you want without the nagging fear of, did someone 'like' that or not?" said Systrom. "Not having feedback is important for Instagram because it is a contrast to the highly pressurized space of a feed where it's all about did this get enough likes, is this good enough?"[9]

Systrom agreed post deletions on their platform were "fairly high" when photos didn't get enough "likes" or users no longer felt the photos accurately reflected their lives. The release of Instagram "Stories" was essentially their way of sealing the deal that "ephemeral sharing" is here to stay. The numbers of users taking advantage of the "Stories" feature is staggering.

Since October 2016, shortly after the release of "Stories," Instagram's daily active user count of the "Stories" feature rose steadily from 100 million in October 2016 to 500 million by January 2019.[10]

---

9   Deepa Seetharaman, "Instagram Unveils Instagram Stories," *Wall Street Journal,* August 2, 2016.

10 "Number of Daily Active Instagram Stories Users from October 2016 to January 2019 (In Millions)," *Statista,* 2019.

Number of Daily Active Instagram Stories Users (in millions)

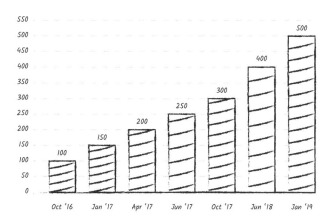

The staggering popularity of Instagram "Stories" confirmed Systrom was right: users, especially younger ones, often preferred to post some things without the pressure of constantly seeking social validation.

The numbers confirm teens' preferences. In the fall 2016 survey "Taking Stock with Teens," Piper Jaffray ranked top social media platforms among teens: Snapchat (35 percent), Instagram (24 percent), Twitter (13 percent), Facebook (13 percent), and Pinterest (1 percent).[11]

By the fall 2018 survey, the numbers had swung: Snapchat

---

11   "Piper Jaffray 32nd Semi-Annual Taking Stock with Teens Survey," *Piper Jaffray Sr. Research Analysts,* Fall 2016.

(46 percent), Instagram (32 percent), Twitter (6 percent), Facebook (5 percent), and Pinterest (1 percent).[12]

Top Social Media Platforms Among Teens

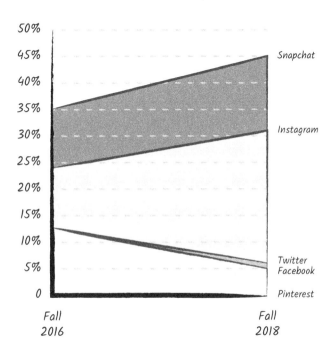

Snapchat and Instagram have grown with teens, at the expense of platforms where content is much more permanent in nature. It's encouraging to see "Stories" running away with the hearts of teens, as this feature focuses around sharing ephemeral posts, while Facebook, Twit-

---

12   "Piper Jaffray 36th Semi-Annual Taking Stock with Teens Survey," *Piper Jaffray Sr. Research Analysts,* Fall 2018.

ter, and traditional Instagram posts are oriented much more around vanity metrics of "likes," comments, and shares or retweets.

An article in the *Guardian* further described the phenomenon. "Beyond the design of the app, there's the unique culture that's grown up around it. Nobody wants a sad profile of pictures that no one has 'liked.'"[13]

If the trend of deleting posts (leading to declines in user-generated content) triggered a swing away from "like-caused" anxiety, I see that as encouragement that people are using more online features that take away the pressure to perform.

UNLIKABLE TRENDS

The second feature Instagram is now testing to take off the social pressure of social media is private "like" counts. Jane Manchun Wong, a tech blogger and researcher known for uncovering new app features before they go public, posted about an unreleased Instagram test on Twitter in April 2019. She posted Instagram screenshots that looked different from what Instagram users are accustomed to seeing on their posts: the posts were missing the "like" count, and instead had a line of text

---

13 Alex Hern, "Why Instagram Would Rather Posts Disappear Than Be Deleted by Users," *The Guardian*, May 30, 2017.

that read, "liked by [username] and *others*." Wong also included Instagram's new tagline for the change: "We want your followers to focus on what you share, not how many likes your posts get."[14]

The feature was rolled out to select Canadian users in May 2019. While "like" counts are now hidden to audiences, users can still click into their own posts and see the list of people who "liked" it, though they won't see the total number of "likes." At the feature's release, the head of Instagram, Adam Mosseri, said, "We don't want Instagram to feel like a competition. We want to make it a less pressurized environment."[15]

---

14   Jane Manchun Wong, Twitter post, April 18, 2019, 1:13PM.

15   Adina Bresge, "Instagram Making 'Like' Counts Private for Some Canadian Users," *Canadian Press,* May 1, 2019.

That may be the public-facing reason for the change, but I think it is simply another reaction to declines in user-generated content among Instagram's core product, traditional posts of photos and videos, as users continue to delete posts with insufficient "likes." By removing "like" counts from public view, Instagram likely hopes that users will post more content that is permanent in nature. These platforms want users' content to stick around, so that there are plenty of posts to consume.

To me, Instagram's developments—"Stories" and private "like" metrics—are encouraging because they were driven by users. But I don't believe for a second that they are introducing these features solely to promote better mental health and less obsessive behavior among their users. On the contrary, these adapted features are in direct response to changes in user behavior, and are designed to keep users coming back, and—most importantly—posting their own content. I feel the true motivations of Instagram and other platforms are to attract and retain daily and monthly active users. As Instagram has seen their user base, and especially younger users, beginning to reject some of the features that promote vanity metrics and social validation, they've tweaked their offerings accordingly.

As social media platforms rely on user-generated content to keep users engaged, we're seeing them grapple with questions of what to curate. Controversial content, in particular, brings large numbers of viewers and users onto platforms. A 2019 article by Mark Bergen in *Bloomberg* describes how YouTube made a goal to hit a billion hours of viewing per day (a goal the company hit in 2016), and in the process allowed toxic content to run wild.[16] The content drove engagement—the highest currency for a social media company—so executives and the CEO ignored warnings and internal proposals for how YouTube could better curate content for viewers.

YouTube's problem, which is shared by many social media platforms, is sparking conversation around freedom of expression and the role social media should play in regulating it. In response to issues of unchecked content, YouTube's CEO Susan Wojcicki compared the video service to a library. The comparison doesn't account for what the algorithms choose to serve up to viewers.

"The massive 'library,' generated by users with little editorial oversight, is bound to have untrue nonsense," wrote Bergen. "YouTube's problem is that it allows the nonsense to flourish. And, in some cases, through its

---

16   Mark Bergen, "YouTube Executives Ignored Warnings, Letting Toxic Videos Run Rampant," *Bloomberg,* April 2, 2019.

powerful artificial intelligence system, it even provides the fuel that lets it spread."

The effects of controversial content on user counts can also be problematic in an age when users are increasingly getting their news from social media rather than traditional news outlets. In May 2019, an altered video of Speaker of the House Nancy Pelosi went viral across Facebook. The video had been slowed down and doctored, and led commentators and pundits to discuss whether Pelosi was inebriated or unwell. Despite the fact that the video was proven to be fake (Facebook even admitted it), Facebook initially refused to remove it from their platform.[17]

On May 24, 2019, CNN's Anderson Cooper interviewed Facebook's head of global policy management, Monika Bickert, on the matter. Bickert said, "Anybody who is seeing this video in news feed, anyone who is going to share it to somebody else, anybody who has shared it in the past, they are being alerted that this video is false,"[18] yet couldn't seem to answer the question: why keep it on the platform?

My answer for why Facebook kept it up: because it was

17   Makena Kelly, "Facebook Begins Telling Users Who Try to Share Distorted Nancy Pelosi Video That It's Fake," *The Verge,* May 25, 2019.

18   Anderson Cooper, "Cooper Grills Facebook VP for Keeping Pelosi Video Up," *CNN,* 2019.

viewed millions of times, by millions of people who came to Facebook to view it. The video eventually disappeared with little fanfare a couple of weeks later, but had already accumulated all of those views.

Another troubling statement came later in the interview when Cooper said: "I understand it's a big business to get into of trying to figure out what's true or not, but you're making money by being in the news business. If you can't do it well, shouldn't you just get out of the news business?"

Bickert's reply? "We aren't in the news business. We're in the social media business."

Don't tell that to the 43 percent of adults who get their news from Facebook.[19] The inability to distinguish between what is fake and what is real on social media is worrisome, and as we see in the Pelosi example, it can have real ripple effects that extend beyond social media and into politics.

IT'S A LONELY CYBER WORLD OUT THERE

The pendulum is swinging. People are starting to realize it's not all roses wandering a virtual world on your own. I read an article in *The Atlantic* ("Is Facebook Making Us Lonely?") that perfectly summarizes the scene: "It's a

---

19 John Gramlich, "10 Facts about Americans and Facebook," *Pew Research Center,* May 16, 2019.

lonely business, wandering the labyrinths of our friends' and pseudo-friends' projected identities, trying to figure out what part of ourselves we ought to project, who will listen, and what they will hear."[20]

Online personas are different than real personas, of course, crafted in a way to maximize followers through "likes" and engagement. As users increasingly become disenchanted with heavily curated content online, platforms will continue to adapt. Social media in the future may look different as designers work with people's impulses and—potentially—even step further away from the negative effects of social validation.

I think we'll continue to see growth in tighter, user-to-user communication platforms in the very near future. Features like "Stories" that take the social performance pressure off will also do very well.

People are increasingly seeing a life full of online connections (and devoid of real-life interactions) is not meaningful, and I feel positive about the changes we'll see in platforms as designers take users' evolving needs into consideration.

Privacy and messaging appear to be the future. Mark Zuckerberg said as much in a March 6, 2019 post: "As I

---

20   Stephen Marche, "Is Facebook Making Us Lonely?" *The Atlantic,* May 2012.

think about the future of the internet, I believe a privacy-focused communications platform will become even more important than today's open platforms," Zuckerberg wrote. "I expect future versions of Messenger and WhatsApp to become the main ways people communicate on the Facebook network."[21]

What is interesting to me is whether the public at large will trust Facebook to bring them into this future of privacy-focused platforms, given that it is the platform that's focused on openness, data collection, and sharing.

Of course, the motivation of social media platforms to adapt to users' needs doesn't stem from an altruistic desire to improve users' mental health or the quality of our social engagements. Each new feature or change is designed to keep us captivated by our platform of choice. Why this need to keep us hooked? In the next chapter we'll start to follow the money—and see the hefty returns social media companies are gleaning from our attention.

---

21   Kurt Wagner, "Mark Zuckerberg Believes Facebook's Future Is Private Messaging," *Vox*, March 6, 2019.

CHAPTER FOUR

DOLLARS AND SENSE IN SOCIAL MEDIA

As a child, well before his career in tech, Tristan Harris dabbled as a magician. In a personal essay on his website, he explained that the two fields were not all that dissimilar. "Magicians start by looking for *blind spots, edges, vulnerabilities and limits* of people's perception, so they can influence what people do without them even realizing it. Once you know how to push people's buttons, you can play them like a piano."[1]

Harris isn't the only one considering how the social media industry is playing sleight-of-hand tricks with our brains. We've discussed the fact that the original designers of

---

[1]   Tristan Harris, "How Technology Hijacks People's Minds—from a Magician and Google's Design Ethicist," essay on *TristanHarris.com*, May 19, 2016.

the most popular platforms are aware of the dopamine cycle and its propensity to get us obsessed with what is happening on our feeds. With so many of the original founders now speaking out, it begs the question: why would these platforms design their systems in a way that leads to compulsive and obsessive use? Why would they create designs to hack our brains, only to renounce their own behaviors and platforms years later?

As is the case most of the time, you simply have to follow the money. In the case of these platforms, it isn't just dollars and cents. They also trade in a currency that we know very well: it is you and I, in the form of being daily or monthly active users.

IT DOESN'T ADD UP

We've talked about Snapchat and how it parlayed the non-permanence of its platform (though as we'll learn later, everything online is permanent) into more than 150 million users. But did you know that for every minute you—or anyone else—spend on their platform, you are costing Snapchat money? From 2016 to 2018, Snapchat lost more than $5.2 billion dollars (that's billion with a "b"). In 2017 alone, they lost more than $3.4 billion. Yet, at the end of May 2019, Snapchat was valued at just short of $16 billion (still well below the $28 billion value on its first day in the public market). Similarly, Twitter lost money every year from its IPO in late 2013, until it finally broke through and had a profitable 2018. Even with all those early losses, at the end of May 2019 Twitter was valued around $28 billion dollars.

How are these companies, that showed massive losses over their first years while trading in public markets, so valuable? Simple—it is because of you, me, and everyone else who gets on their platforms and engages with the content on our feeds.

Companies are valued by investors' expectations of future prospects or profitability. Snapchat and Twitter held tremendous value despite having significant losses because investors believed that those companies would be able to turn all of their users into revenue. The word for that is monetization—a term you'll hear a lot about when you follow the companies that rule Silicon Valley.

For social media companies with large user bases, investors are making a bet that the company will turn those users into profits eventually. That's why they give these companies higher values than the pure numbers might dictate at the time—they believe in the future earning potential of that platform's user base.

Twitter has finally turned those users into greater advertising revenue and into profitability, earning more than

$1.2 billion in 2018. They're on track to play out the story that investors want to see.

Facebook and Google (which is technically owned by its parent company, Alphabet) have different stories. Both of these companies have been profitable since they began trading in public markets. Facebook's IPO was in May 2012 and Alphabet's in August 2004. Both showed relatively modest profits in their early years and have continued to grow in profitability over the years.

Still, both Google and Facebook have proven to be more valuable than the average company. Why? Again, because of the vast amounts of daily and active monthly users.

SOCIAL MEDIA MEETS WALL STREET

There is so much value to be gleaned from user data—we'll take an in-depth look at why in the next chapter—and as a result, markets measure the value of these social media platforms not just by assessing their profitability, but by tallying us up in the form of daily and monthly active users. As we've seen with Snapchat and Twitter, being profitable is not a prerequisite to holding tremendous value. Your presence on a particular platform builds up additional market value for that company, because your participation adds to that company's data set. Due to the huge volume of consumer data that can be gleaned from platforms with large user bases, profitable social media platforms are valued much more highly than the average company in the eyes of investors.

Price-to-earnings ratios are a simple way that markets and investors benchmark the value of companies. The price-to-earnings ratio definitely isn't the only type of measure that financial analysts will use to evaluate a company, but it is very helpful when comparing relative value. Without getting into too much detail, a higher price-to-earnings ratio means that the investment community has placed higher expectations on the future prospects or profitability of a given company.

Facebook and Google (Alphabet) have traditionally traded well above the price-to-earnings ratio of the S&P 500. The S&P 500 is an index of 500 large US companies that is often used as a barometer for the stock market as a whole. In recent years, Facebook's price-to-earnings ratio has been as high as more than five times that of the S&P 500, while Google's ratio has been more than double that of the index. Simply put, this tells us that these companies are seen as being much more valuable than the "average" company.

The point is this: investors place a premium on companies like Facebook and Google versus other large corporations because of the immense number of users on these plat-forms. Investors think they can drive more future value from all that available data.

DOES "THE MARKET" CARE ABOUT PRIVACY?

One of the risks, of course, of social media platforms collecting so much data on users is that it leaves us vulner-able to privacy violations in the case of a security breach or scandal. This isn't just a worry for the future—it's a reality in our lives today. In their first-quarter earnings statement for 2019, Facebook deducted $3 billion from their profits because they were anticipating a fine from the Federal Trade Commission (FTC) for breaches of privacy and user data made by the platform.

This pending fine reduced the company's earnings, of course—but how much do our security concerns play into these companies' valuations in the market? Not much, it seems.

Facebook's monthly active user count increased to 2.38 billion, up 8 percent year-over-year versus the same time in 2018. Facebook earned $15.08 billion in revenue in the quarter, which was a year-over-year increase of 26 percent. Its earnings per share were $0.85—which didn't meet estimates of $1.63—but that was only because they had removed the pending $3 billion FTC fine. Without that charge, earnings per share would have been $1.89.[2]

In its earnings release, Facebook said, "In the first quarter of 2019, we reasonably estimated a probable loss and recorded an accrual of $3.0 billion in connection with the inquiry of the FTC into our platform and user data practices, which accrual is included in accrued expenses and other current liabilities on our condensed consolidated balance sheet. We estimate that the range of loss in this matter is $3.0 billion to $5.0 billion. The matter remains unresolved, and there can be no assurance as to the timing or the terms of any final outcome."[3]

To sum up: Facebook told the market that it was expecting a very significant fine for privacy issues—to the tune of $3 to $5 billion—yet had an otherwise very successful quarter. So, would the market punish them for the continuing issues with privacy, or reward them for a great financial quarter?

Well, the market responded definitively. Facebook's share price increased by 8.3 percent the day of the earnings release. The market rewarded Facebook for the profits and basically ignored the negativity associated with the

---

2   Josh Constine, "Facebook Reserves $3B for FTC Fine, but Keeps Growing with 2.38B Users in Q1," *TechCrunch,* May 2019.

3   "Facebook Reports First Quarter 2019 Results," Facebook Press Release, April 24, 2019.

impending fine. The increase in Facebook's share price raised the company's value by more than $30 billion.[4]

Facebook Increase in Market Capitalization After Q1 2019 Earnings Release

$30 billion

Anticipated FTC Fine

$3 billion

---

4   "Facebook Market Cap," *Y Charts*, June 4, 2019.

On a broader scale, this is troubling. If privacy transgressions are expected to result in a fine of $3 to $5 billion, but the market rewards them with $30 billion in return, there is very little disincentive for Facebook to shore up its practices. In fact, I'd be willing to bet that Facebook takes that trade every single time. I think Scott Galloway and Kara Swisher said it very well on their podcast *Pivot*: the fine is effectively nothing more than a parking ticket for Facebook and will not dissuade similar behavior in the future.[5]

LEVERAGING ENTERPRISE VALUE

So we've learned that social media companies have a lot of value, as long as they have users. Profitability is nice, but not always needed for these companies to carry significant value in the market. What does this value mean to these companies, and what do they do with it?

When companies like Facebook are valued more by investors than the average company, which has shown to be true, it gives these companies access to cheap capital. Access to cheap capital means that these companies can raise funds much more easily and more cheaply than other companies, which gives them a huge advantage over the competition. With access to cheap capital, com-

---

5   Kara Swisher and Scott Galloway, "The FTC & 'the Algebra of Deterrence,'" *Pivot* (podcast), 2019.

panies have the ability to more easily spur growth by investing funds back into themselves and their products, or often through acquiring other companies.

Acquisitions can play a major part in the growth of a social media organization. By buying other platforms, social media companies can rapidly expand their footprint and their user base. In some cases, they will continue to operate that platform independently. Or, they can consolidate that platform into their own to add new users to their service. In any case, it also allows them to build a deeper profile of those users for the purposes of advertising.

An example here will be helpful. Let's look at how Facebook leveraged its value and access to cheap capital to fuel tremendous growth over recent years.

FACEBOOK'S GROWTH CYCLE

We've previously discussed Facebook's value as a social media company that offered the rare combination of a massive user base alongside profitability. In addition, we noted that Facebook was still much more valuable than the "average" company (represented by the S&P 500). So, how did Facebook leverage all of that value? By making two key acquisitions in the early 2010s that it is now hard to imagine Facebook being without.

In April 2012, just before its initial public offering, Facebook bought a peer-to-peer photo-sharing app called Instagram for $1 billion. At the time of the acquisition, Instagram had about 30 million monthly active users.[6] (Facebook had about 900 million.)[7]

Then, in February 2014, Facebook made another very significant acquisition. It purchased a private messaging platform called WhatsApp for $19 billion. At the time of acquisition, WhatsApp had about 450 million monthly active users[8] while Facebook itself had about 1.2 billion.[9]

These weren't the only acquisitions Facebook has made. The company has acquired around 80 companies since its inception. But I would argue that these two—Instagram and WhatsApp—have been the most significant by far. In fact, I would argue that they've been among the most accretive acquisitions ever completed. In mid-2018, Bloomberg estimated that Instagram would be worth more than $100 billion as a standalone company[10] (greater than 100 times the purchase price), while Mark Zuckerberg announced that WhatsApp had grown to 1.5

6   Bruce Upbin, "Facebook Buys Instagram for $1 Billion. Smart Arbitrage," *Forbes*, April 9, 2012.

7   "Number of Monthly Active Facebook Users Worldwide as of 1st Quarter 2019," *Statista*, 2019.

8   Josh Constine, "WhatsApp Hits 1.5 Billion Monthly Users. $19B? Not So Bad." *TechCrunch*, 2018.

9   "Number of Monthly Active Facebook Users Worldwide as of 1st Quarter 2019," *Statista*, 2019.

10 Emily McCormick, "Instagram Is Estimated to Be Worth More Than $100 Billion," *Bloomberg*, June 25, 2018.

billion monthly active users by the end of 2017, more than 3.3 times what it had at the time of acquisition.[11]

As we'll learn next chapter, Facebook has since used common user profile information—namely, email addresses and phone numbers—to consolidate the user profiles of people who are on one or more of these platforms. By consolidating a user's Facebook, Instagram, and WhatsApp profiles, Facebook is able to offer advertisers stronger user profiles. Of course, deeper information on users increases the accuracy of advertisements to those users.

Early in 2019, Mark Zuckerberg took this next step when he announced plans to consolidate WhatsApp, Facebook Messenger, and Instagram Messenger, citing encryption concerns as a motivation. He claimed the merger will ensure everyone's personal data on these services—messages, photos, videos, voice messages, documents, attachments, any calls that you make—are going to be encrypted across all platforms.

The *New York Times* described this as "a move that will bring together three of the world's largest messaging networks, which between them have more than 2.6 billion

---

11   Josh Constine, "WhatsApp Hits 1.5 Billion Monthly Users. $19B? Not So Bad," *TechCrunch*, 2018.

users, allowing people to communicate across the platforms for the first time."[12]

While that may be true, make no mistake: this increases their profile of you and consolidates your personal data across all platforms. This takes the choice away from consumers who may want to keep this data separate, and raises concerns for the future of privacy and data sharing.

The *New York Times* article continued with a more harrowing, and realistic, view of what this move meant for Facebook's users: "The move has the potential to redefine how billions of people use the apps to connect with one another while strengthening Facebook's grip on users, raising antitrust, privacy and security questions. It also underscores how Mr. Zuckerberg is imposing his authority over units he once vowed to leave alone."

The move toward consolidation has not been popular even within Facebook's environs. Kevin Systrom and Mike Krieger, co-founders of Instagram, left Facebook late in 2018, following the high-profile departure of WhatsApp's co-founder Jan Koum. There's been wide speculation that all three execs had concerns about the merging of platforms and the related effects on data privacy.

---

12   Mike Isaac, "Zuckerberg Plans to Integrate WhatsApp, Instagram and Facebook Messenger," *New York Times*, January 25, 2019.

Facebook has shown to be able to leverage its sheer size and value to continue to fuel its growth, both organically and through these key acquisitions. Facebook's move to consolidate several of its platforms will be a topic of discussion in the coming months and years, as there are mounting calls from the public and government officials to break the company up, citing antitrust concerns. But there's no denying that Facebook has been able to use this cycle to grow significantly; at the end of May 2019, the company was valued at more than $500 billion, far more than the $104 billion valuation the company priced its shares at ahead of its IPO in 2012.

USERS > ETHICS

So, what does this tell us? There is tremendous value in having vast amounts of users on these platforms. Users make these platforms much more valuable than the average company, and the platforms have been able to use that value to fuel significant growth and quickly expand their footprints.

The value created by user counts, in the form of daily and monthly active users, incentivizes platforms to acquire and retain users at all costs. This can even result in design choices that are ethically questionable at best. Generally speaking, whenever these platforms find themselves in the news for questionable tactics, you can usually trace it back to their attempts to gain more users, or to retain existing users. We see this come to life in the design features we've discussed that drive the dopamine-driven cycles that keep us coming back to the platform, as well as massive efforts to combat declines in user-generated content. In short, those platforms will always be driven to promote features and activities that bring users, even if those tactics cross ethical lines.

To this point, we've focused on the features of the platforms themselves that have been designed to exploit us into obsessive behavior to keep us coming back. Now, let's discuss what happens once we are on the platforms. This is where much of the manipulative activity happens. In general, manipulative features are driven by third parties that are the customers of the platforms: advertising companies. Combined with the reach and targeting power of the social networks and the vast amounts of data they collect from us, these platforms and their customers (advertisers) have the power to influence our behavior in ways never seen before.

Facebook and Google have built the world's best advertising platforms, because they dominate the world's consumer data; no other companies (besides Amazon and maybe Apple) come close. This is the other reason that platforms are so motivated to attract, and retain, users—to serve the needs of third-party advertisers. By bringing in more user data every single second of every day, these social media giants are positioned to be far and away the best advertising platforms. Facebook and Google offer advertisers not only a massive audience, but also the ability to create more captive audiences through detailed targeting based on our data and user profiles.

The days of companies just putting ads on TV and hoping to see results, but not being able to attract the right customers in a targeted way, are over. That was simply a very inefficient approach. Facebook and Google are able to offer advertisers so much more precision with every advertising dollar that goes out.

Enter the algorithms. Jaron Lanier might have said it best: "You are being subtly manipulated by algorithms that are watching everything you do constantly and then sending you changes in your media feed, in your diet, that are calculated to adjust you slightly to the liking of some unseen advertiser."[13]

Let's look at how it works.

---

13 "Jaron Lanier Interview on How Social Media Ruins Your Life," YouTube video, posted by *Channel 4 News*, June 15, 2018.

CHAPTER FIVE

FEEDING THE BEAST

A few years back I had my eyes set on a pair of new Bose headphones.

I had no idea the headphones had their eyes on me, too.

I started shopping around on various websites, looking at prices but not making a commitment to purchase. Pretty soon I noticed that everywhere else I went online, the headphones were there.

I went to the ESPN site to read some sports news and boom; an ad appeared for the headphones. I checked the weather site and a headphone ad hovered above the five-day forecast like an incoming cold front. I went to my Instagram feed, and Bose was there. I had no idea at the time what was going on, but it started getting creepy:

the headphones followed me across all my social media platforms and all my browser activity, tempting me to buy them.

Most people have experienced a product that seems to follow them around the internet. It's not magic; it's an intentional marketing move. I had already shown interest in that set of headphones, and Bose was simply pushing me to complete the purchase—to close the sale. This is a type of subtle manipulation called "conversion" in digital marketing. The algorithms in place to make this all happen are mind-bogglingly complicated, and extremely effective.

In this case, I as the customer had sought out that product in the first place; the brand already knew I was interested. What about brands or products that I wasn't even aware of yet? How do they entice me (and you) to learn about and purchase other products I might be interested in? Social media feeds and website ad space serve up ads tailored specifically to your interests.

To make the most of the ads companies put in front of you, they have to know you're interested in a particular product or category. Where do they get that information?

Virtually every brand tracks what you view on their company website, of course, but many of them also advertise with Google and Facebook, who give the brands the ability to target you because of the data they have available. As you engage with content, click links posted by friends and leave comments, social media platforms are collecting information about who you're connected to, how you spend your time and money, and what brands you might be aligned with.

This is where the stickiness of social media serves the needs of its true customers: companies that advertise on their platforms. We've already talked about the importance of users from an investor standpoint, but companies that spend their advertising dollars on these platforms are just as interested in these platforms not only having a large number of engaged users, but also having a lot of data on those users so they can better target them with the right ads at the right time.

When we refer to "manipulation," we're talking about the subtle nudges you receive from third-party brands that are trying to get you to take an action on their advertisements. They want a click, a purchase, a "like," or some other action on their content. It is truly a perfect marriage, because the massive platforms have tremendous amounts of user data and profiles that greatly increase the likelihood of a given user taking that action. Algorithms track everything you do on the platform and then serve up advertisements from third parties that are most likely to be of interest to you.

Up to this point, we've discussed how social media platforms design their features to keep you active and engaged on their platform. Ultimately, the actions they're really driving—beyond your "likes" and comments on your friends' content—is your engagement with ads. Third-party advertisers are the "man behind the curtain": they're the ones trying to elicit a response from you.

As a result, Facebook and Google have far and away built the best advertising platforms ever seen. This is big business—Facebook earned more than $55 billion in advertising revenues in 2018 alone.[1] Google's 2018 advertising revenues were more than $118 billion.[2] Not to be ignored, Twitter earned $2.6 billion in advertising rev-

---

[1]   "Annual Report 2018," Facebook, 2018.

[2]   "Form 10-K 2018," Alphabet, 2018.

enue in 2018,[3] while Snapchat earned about $1.2 billion in revenue that year (per its annual report, 99 percent of Snapchat's revenue comes from advertisers).[4]

Approximate Social Media Advertising Revenues by Day (2018)

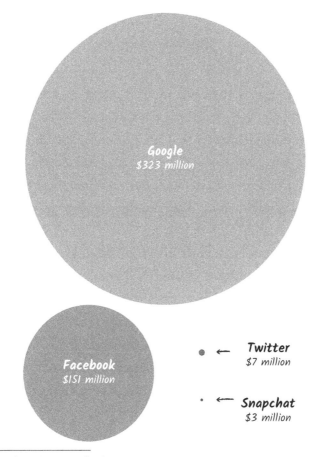

Google
$323 million

Facebook
$151 million

← Twitter
$7 million

← Snapchat
$3 million

---

3   "Annual Report 2018," Twitter, 2018.

4   "Annual Report 2018," Snap Inc., 2018.

We love that social media platforms are free and convenient, but it's important to understand the real hidden costs in the data they collect and the ways they thrive from user engagement.

Hint: if you don't pay for it, *you* are the product.

IT'S ALL ABOUT ALGORITHMS

You're the one bringing value to that platform in the form of your behavior and your interests. As you click on what you like, you give social media platforms information about market trends and purchase motivations. The platform's goal is to expand the network to include as many user touchpoints as possible, so they can then engage you with ads that are most likely to entice a purchase.

It's actually relatively simple: social media platforms aren't viable without people; they need you, and they use reward loops to drive you where they want you to go. Platforms are essentially a canvas for advertising, and they constantly curate and edit content based on your interests. This allows brands that buy ad space through these platforms to target you with content they know you'll find engaging.

They do this through algorithms. Here's a simple way to think about them: running an algorithm is like the process of picking a movie to watch with someone. When my wife and I went on our first date, I didn't know her that well, so I picked a movie that was "safe." I'm sure I settled on a nice romantic comedy. As we continued to date and eventually married, I've been able to collect many more data points on my wife. Now, if we decide to watch a movie, I'm in a much better position to choose something that I know she'll like. For our movie nights, perhaps I'll first look at all the movies playing in the theater. Then I might consider having a night in, and expand my selection to include movies on demand.

Then I can bring other data points into my decision-making process: Does she like Drama? Action? Horror? What happened this week—is she more likely to want an intense movie, or will she want to unwind and have some laughs? What are the last movies we watched? Has she told me there's a certain movie she wants to see? Have any friends recommended a movie to me or to her?

This is how social media populates your feed. Over time, they gather more and more information about you to better understand you. Recency is important: what have you been up to lately?

The more active you are on social media, the more information you provide to them. If they understand you better, they are more likely to put stories, articles, and ads in front of you that will elicit a response.

That's why they spend so much time, money, and effort on grabbing and keeping your attention. They want to pick the perfect movie for you.

Scott Galloway, a professor of marketing at NYU Stern (and a hero of mine), appropriately calls algorithms "Benjamin Button" systems, named after the Brad Pitt movie about a character who begins his life as an old man and gets younger and younger throughout the story. In the context of social media, a Benjamin Button is characterized as "aging in reverse, an algorithm that improves with use," he wrote in an article for *Gartner*.[5] Every single Google search you make makes its algorithms better. Every time you log on to Facebook, retweet on Twitter, or select one of Spotify's preset music playlists, the algorithm sees, and it gets better and better at feeding you content.

---

5   Scott Galloway, "There Is Another," *Gartner,* May 11, 2018.

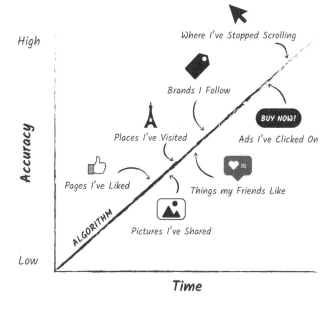

The more you engage with content, the more the algorithm learns about your preferences, your behavior, and even your spending habits. In his book *Ten Reasons for Deleting Your Social Media Accounts Right Now,* Jaron Lanier describes how algorithms loop into our dopamine cycle with variable rewards:

> The algorithm is trying to capture the perfect parameters for manipulating the brain, while the brain, in order to seek out deeper meaning, is changing in response to the algorithm's experiments...Because the stimuli from the algorithm doesn't mean anything, because they genuinely are random, the brain isn't responding to anything real,

but to a fiction. That process—of becoming hooked on an elusive mirage—is addiction.[6]

As an algorithm succeeds in keeping you engaged with a platform, you grow that platform's footprint. Think of when you used your Facebook login to connect to your Spotify account or other third-party sites: each time you connect one platform with another site or service, you potentially give the social media platform access to your behavior on other sites across the internet.

The ultimate goal of social media platforms is to grow their ecosystems with more people, more touchpoints, and ultimately, more data. As you've seen already, they leverage basic human behavior and the dopamine cycle to drive obsession and engagement. When they keep users clicking on more and more things, they also keep those users connecting to more and more data.

JUST KEEP CLICKING

In July 2016, Instagram (which was acquired by Facebook in 2012, remember) changed their feed organization from chronological to algorithmic, and this simple move allowed them to do a better job of grabbing our atten-

---

6   Zoe Williams, "Ten Arguments for Deleting Your Social Media Accounts Right Now by Jaron Lanier—Review," *The Guardian,* May 30, 2018.

tion, and then to leverage data about user preferences to streamline marketing efforts.

In the older chronological version of the feed, the newest posts went to the top. This presented an issue from Facebook's perspective: what if the newest posts weren't the most interesting ones? As soon as users disengage and close the app, the platform loses the opportunity to gather more data.

With a chronological feed, posts that were most likely to engage users could be buried twentieth on the list. If a user doesn't open the app in a day or two, engaging content gets pushed even farther down. That means there'd be a luck factor involved with engaging the user. Remember; if they're not engaging you, you're less likely to be building value for them.

Instagram and Facebook use a mix of criteria to determine the order of a feed. Instagram prioritizes posts that they predict will interest you, based on your previous behavior, followed by the recency of the item. Lastly, they consider the closeness of relationships in what rises to the top of your feed.[7]

Adam Mosseri, who led Facebook's News Feeds and is now the head of Instagram, did an excellent job explain-

---

7   Josh Constine, "How Instagram's Algorithm Works," *TechCrunch*, June 1, 2018.

ing the platform's algorithms in the video "How Does the Facebook News Feed Ranking Work?"[8] In the video, he explained that Facebook's algorithms prioritize items in your News Feed in the following order:

1. Inventory—All the news items you haven't seen
2. Signals—Information we have available (how old a story is, who posted it, what is the signal on your phone)
3. Predictions—How likely are you to comment, share, or hide?

This all rolls up into a relevancy score, and posts are ordered in what the algorithm believes best matches your interests.

As we've seen, algorithms changed the playing field, as platforms use all of the data they know about you to make predictions on what you are most likely to engage with, and then track whether you engage or not. If you "like" or comment or share a post, you've validated your usage. The algorithm improves the more often you engage with content, and it moves the most relevant stuff to the top of your feed—advertising, messages from friends, any pages that you chose to follow. Algorithms choose what you see and in what order, to keep your interest piqued.

8   Adam Mosseri, "How the Facebook Algorithm Works," *YouTube*, October 11, 2018.

The effects of algorithms extend beyond advertising. Social platforms have even changed the way we receive our news. Because of the information they collect, social platforms have the ability to understand you better and put more relevant news in front of you. As previously mentioned, the number of people using Facebook as their primary news source is staggering—around 43 percent, according to the Pew Research Center.[9] Additionally, 21 percent get news from YouTube, 12 percent from Twitter, 8 percent from Instagram, and 5 percent from Snapchat.[10] Facebook, Google, and other social platforms know best what you're interested in, what you want to learn about the world, and what you want to buy.

---

9   John Gramlich, "10 Facts About Americans and Facebook," *Pew Research Center,* May 16, 2019.

10   Katerina Eva Matsa and Elisa Shearer, "News across Social Media Platforms 2018," *Pew Research Center,* September 10, 2018.

Where do people get their news from?

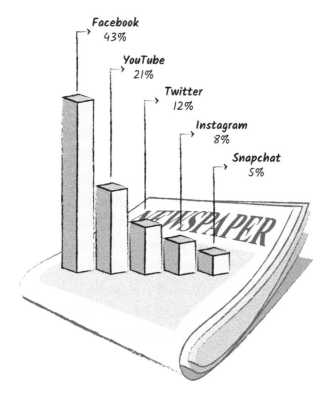

Algorithms also create an interesting dynamic for those who are chasing "likes" and other vanity metrics. If you post your own user-generated content and other people don't engage with your posts, you're much less likely to get to the top of the feed. And if you don't get to the top of the feed, it's going to be hard to get "likes." Attention becomes a chicken-and-egg problem: when your content isn't "liked," it falls farther down the feed, making it far less likely that you'll get more "likes." I think the risk here is that we'll continue to see more extreme content because it is more likely to grab attention (whether positive or negative). Imagine the effect these algorithmic feeds have on teens chasing "likes," and how it might affect what they post, as well as drive the frequency with which they check the popularity of their posts. Again, all the more reason to keep coming back to the platform and to post content that is likely to get attention.

DATA COLLECTION AGENCIES

So, algorithms are extremely effective in keeping us engaged on the various platforms and serving us advertisements in our News Feeds or on websites that are likely to elicit a response. In order for those ads to be effective in converting us, manipulating us to take a desired action, these platforms have to get to know us—what we like, what we're interested in, and what we tend to respond to. By now we know that every time we click, "like," leave a comment, or share something, we have told the platform, "More of that, please!" Let's look at some other ways that these platforms are collecting data on us to better serve the needs of their customers.

FACEBOOK KNOWS YOUR BEST FRIENDS

You already know that Facebook algorithms track "likes," shares, and comments. The algorithms also take this to the next level by ranking the amount of engagement signaled by each kind of behavior.

The highest-ranked interaction is comments, followed by reactions ("likes"), then replies to comments, and finally, sharing links over Messenger.[11] By ranking the quality of your interactions with other people's posts, Facebook can pick out who you pay the most attention to online.

Even if you don't click, the algorithm still learns about you simply by tracking your scrolling habits. Each time you pause on a story or post, Facebook knows you're taking time to check it out, even if you choose not to engage. That is how powerful the algorithms are—they are able to recognize that you've stopped scrolling somewhere in your News Feed and can then prioritize similar posts in the future.

THE BUSINESS OF "LIKES"

Another way Facebook creates robust data sets is by tracking "likes" of businesses pages. Initially, companies created Facebook pages primarily to grow brand awareness. But as users "like" brands and visit their pages, Facebook is able to gather precious information about

---

11   Shannon Tien, "How the Facebook Algorithm Works and How You Can Make It Work for You," *Hootsuite,* April 25, 2018.

how users are navigating to brand pages, how much time they spend there, and what they view.

When you scroll through your Facebook feed and "like" a brand page from Ikea, you instantly link all of your behavior—from your visit to the Ikea Facebook page to your shopping time on Ikea.com—to Facebook's powerful collection of advertising data.

ONE LOGIN, ONE DATA MINE

You don't even have to technically be on one of the platforms for them to be collecting more data on you.

Have you ever used the "Login with Facebook" option when signing up for a new service, like Spotify, Airbnb, Expedia, or the *New York Times*? If so, you are likely giving Facebook more information, even though you aren't technically on their platform. They don't stop at their own platform when mining for data points about you, and a great many services and websites offer the option of signing in with your Facebook account.

Sounds great, right? Fewer passwords to remember and a single sign-in experience is appealing. But think for a moment what happens next—you could be sharing what you are listening to, where you are vacationing, where you are staying, or what you are reading.

A recent study, "No Boundaries for Facebook Data," looked at the consequences of a single login. When you use your social media profile to grant access to a website, you're also granting permission to third parties who may be embedded—and invisible—on that site.[12] "Hidden third-party trackers," the researchers found, "can also use Facebook Login to de-anonymize users for targeted advertising."

Wired described the study in similar terms:

> The researchers found that sometimes when users grant permission for a website to access their Facebook profile, third-party trackers embedded on the site are getting that data, too. That can include a user's name, email address, age, birthday, and other information, depending on what info the original site requested to access. The study found that this particular breed of tracking script is present on 434 of the web's top one million websites, though not all of them are querying Facebook data from the API—the researchers only confirmed that such a script was present.[13]

In addition to opening yourself up to advertising, which can be annoying but isn't generally harmful, you may be

---

12   Steven Englehardt, Gunes Acar, and Arvind Narayanan, "No Boundaries for Facebook Data: Third-Party Trackers Abuse Facebook Login," *Freedom to Tinker*, April 18, 2018.

13   Louise Matsakis, "The Security Risks of Logging In with Facebook," *Wired*, April 19, 2018.

putting your data at risk by introducing more third parties to the equation.

While you may trust Facebook's security, or even the security of the site you're logging into, using your Facebook login gives the same permissions to third-party sites that you may not even be aware of. These third parties can then go on to use or even sell your personal data.

Is this sounding familiar?

Hello, Cambridge Analytica, the political data firm that was able to obtain unauthorized information belonging to up to 87 million people because users unknowingly shared their Facebook data with a personality quiz app called "thisisyourdigitallife." Even more troubling, the data firm was able to obtain not only information on the people who used the Facebook quiz app, but also information on the friends who were in their networks. That is how the 270,000 users who answered the quiz turned into more than 87 million total users who were affected.[14] Cambridge Analytica went on to use that data to target political ads to these users during the 2016 presidential election.

Indeed, the single-login trend is widely visible throughout

---

14   Izzy Lapowsky, "Facebook Exposed 87 Million Users to Cambridge Analytica," *Wired*, April 4, 2018.

the online world. When Spotify launched in the US in 2011, it required users to sign up with Facebook. Spotify would then post to Facebook, telling your friends what you are listening to.

When large security breaches happen, such as the breach in September 2018 that exposed the personal data of 50 million Facebook users, they potentially leak not only the user's Facebook information, but the data from any additional sites that have been connected by a Facebook login.

Remember, when you log in somewhere using Facebook, you are introducing many more variables and potential exposure of your personal data—all tying back to your Facebook profile.

NOT-SO-PRIVATE MESSAGES

Another way Facebook can potentially collect data from users who aren't even on its platform is with businesses that are starting to use its Messenger for the live chats on their sites. While the Facebook logo is present on these chat windows, the business can create their own branded skin on the window, so most consumers don't realize they're chatting in a Facebook product.

Facebook then of course can glean user data from the chats, including name, gender, and location of the user.

It improves customer experience but is also another open pipeline for platforms to potentially "listen in" on your life.

POWERFUL PROFILES

After these platforms collect data about user interests and behaviors, they are able to create profiles of user groups. These profiles allow companies to compare data from similar users: they group by age, gender, interests, and what users click on. Profiles help companies predict what users will like, based on behavior and interests gathered from similar users.

Our engagement in social media sucks us into an online marketing orbit. The more data that platforms and vendors are able to collect from us, the more insight they have on potential customers with similar interests and behaviors.

If Joe's Bike Shop is pushing a new model, they can look at profiles of consumers on social media and choose who to target with ads on the platforms. If they know you're interested in a certain bike magazine and tend to "like" content of certain bike brands, they are able to ascertain that you are very likely to be a biking fan. They don't have to rely on only your activity—they can look to what your cycling friends have "liked" and purchased to predict what products you might buy.

It's easy to see how robust profiles can be made from platforms like Facebook, where people are constantly engaging with their friends about what they like. But as Charlie Grinnell, CEO of the digital intelligence firm RightMetric, points out, some platforms like Instagram or WhatsApp require an email and phone number to sign up. These platforms are not as old as Facebook, and as he told me in an interview, they "don't have the same deep trove of data that you have on a Facebook account where people have been happily entering in who they're friends with and where they went to school and what hockey teams they like."[15]

Of course, there's a hack for that. Advertisers who want to splash ads on Instagram purchase that ad space through the Facebook Ads Manager. Facebook can take all the data points they have on the individual user, you, and cross-reference them with your Instagram account.

How do they do that? As discussed in the previous chapter, Facebook is like the Walmart of the online world. They currently own WhatsApp, Facebook, Facebook Messenger, and Instagram (among others). They made strategic acquisitions to expand their footprint and have built substantial value in the process. This also means that they are able to link and consolidate

---

15   Charlie Grinnell, personal interview with the author, February 13, 2019.

profiles across their platforms. Through common email addresses or phone numbers associated with individual profiles, user data from Facebook can be linked to Instagram, WhatsApp, and virtually any Facebook platform or service connected to the same email address or phone number. The resulting combined data sets from all these user connections make their advertising profiles even stronger, and brands can target users more effectively.

HOW TARGETING WORKS

Now that the companies have engaged you, collected immense amounts of data on you, and consolidated all of the information they have on you across all of their platforms, they enable brands to target you in many different ways. This is where the rubber truly meets the road—how are you being targeted with those ads that populate your feeds and websites you visit? We'll hone in on Facebook's Ad Manager here, but Google has similar mechanisms through its own ad platform. Twitter, Snapchat, and others have similar services, but Facebook and Google are clearly the front-runners here with the vast amounts of data they have.

As an example, let's say a sports apparel business is looking to create targeted ads on Instagram. Let's look at the ways that company can target us with those ads.

First, they can target us based upon demographic information and interests or affinities. Facebook lets advertisers target by Location, Demographics, Interests, Behaviors (past purchases or device usage), and Connections (those that are connected to their brand).[16] While the company can't drill all the way down to a specific person or small group that would expose personal information, they can target across these categories in a very granular way. Want to reach college-educated males aged 21–34 in the Bay Area that are fans of the NFL? Facebook's got your back.

Second, Facebook allows targeting based on a list that the advertising company itself provides, perhaps from an email newsletter mailing list, a customer relationship management system, or a list of people who have visited that company's website or used its app. That business can upload a list of user information to Facebook Ad Manager. Facebook will cross-reference the list against its user base. The results will come back, and a certain amount of the people on the list will have an Instagram account associated with the same email. Some will be men, some will be women. Following "likes" and preferences from Facebook data, the business can also identify that some of the men like the Seattle Seahawks. Some of the women live in Massachusetts and follow the NFL page—likely they are Patriots fans. "You can then take those prefer-

16   "About," Facebook Business, 2019.

ences and tendencies and deploy them on Instagram," Grinnell explained, "and they've now extended that out to businesses: businesses are able to export a spreadsheet of their email lists, upload them to Facebook, and create an audience to target based on those email addresses."

The sports apparel business now knows exactly what ad to place for each user, customized with their favorite teams from their geographic region.

Finally, Facebook enables advertisers to create what are called Lookalike Audiences. Let's say the company has a list of email addresses from its best customers and would like to find and advertise to more people who are likely to share some of the same characteristics. The company can upload its customer list into Facebook, which will then match those emails to the users on its platforms and look for common demographics, interests, and behaviors. Facebook will then find other user profiles that share the same attributes and allow the apparel company to send its targeted ads to that new audience.

The next time you visit your News Feed, rest assured that whatever advertisements you see are coming from one of these sources. There is one more very powerful element of Facebook's ad platform that goes beyond simply show-ing us the ad—they want to help companies close sales. To the bottom of the sales funnel we go.

CONVERTING PROFILES TO PURCHASES

Back to the headphones that followed me around Facebook. Since it's equal parts fascinating and creepy, let's briefly look at the mechanics of how that works. Enter Facebook Pixel.

In Facebook's own promotional words, "The Facebook Pixel is an analytics tool that allows you to measure the effectiveness of your advertising by understanding the actions people take on your website. You can use the pixel data to make sure your ads are being shown to the right people, build advertising audiences, and unlock additional Facebook advertising tools."[17]

What is it exactly? The Pixel tool is code embedded into websites that links your online behavior with your Facebook profile by syncing with Facebook cookies residing in your browser. Start watching a video on a site and leave? Put something in a shopping cart and then abandon it (a nightmare for e-commerce companies)? Next time you browse Facebook, Instagram, or Messenger, presto! Your past returns in a conveniently placed ad with an easy link to lure you back in.

Google uses a similar tool, Google Analytics, to tailor ads across all kinds of websites. When I'm signed into

---

17   Perry Marshall, "How to Use the Two Greatest Superpowers of Facebook's Analytics Tool," *Entrepreneur,* November 1, 2017.

my Chrome browser, Google knows everything I'm up to. Those ads follow me everywhere, from my favorite sports pages to my news sites.

Marketers consider shares, "likes," and comments to be "vanity" metrics because they're generally not as concerned with the popularity of their own posts—they're much more interested in how often they convert your attention into sales.

Google Analytics and Facebook Pixel give marketers conversion metrics to show how effective their ads are in getting an action from you, whether it's clicking on something to get more information or finishing the sale. It's a super-efficient way to target and retarget you with ads.

ARE ALGORITHMS EVIL?

Here's the thing though. We'll always be exposed to ads, so why not have those ads be for things that we are actually interested in? Algorithms are not inherently evil; they are just a set of rules that tell a computer how to perform a particular task. They have many different applications, but a lot of social media and e-commerce platforms use algorithms to analyze your data and "personalize" what you see.

I'm actually (relatively) thankful for algorithms when I

scroll through my own feeds, because they help to prioritize the posts I'm interested in. There is just so much content and information out there, that I don't think any of us could reasonably seek everything out without their help.

But it's important to understand, too, how these companies grab our attention, collect our data, and use that data to target us with ads. These are the trade-offs we make with free platforms. Social media companies need to make money, and their currency is our attention.

Where we have to be much more careful is with the attention-grabbing nature of the platforms we use, the dopamine-driven reward cycles that keep us coming back, and the advertisements that we see across our News Feeds and websites we visit. These are all forms of manipulative activities: they are steering us to the desired outcome of the platform or the third party. They want us to come to their platforms, stay awhile, visit often, and take action on ads.

If there has been a positive to the seemingly nonstop reports of user data and privacy concerns on these platforms (mostly Facebook), it is that the vast majority of users now understand that the platforms are not truly free. The Cambridge Analytica scandal specifically shone a light on just how these platforms truly work, and who they work for.

I use some of these platforms actively, but I am also acutely aware of the fact the algorithms are at work. I'm consciously choosing to trade a few subliminally induced impulse clicks and purchases in exchange for a more relevant, personalized feed.

But I'm an adult. Kids don't yet have the agency to choose those tradeoffs, and they won't have the self-awareness to recognize when algorithms or app designs are pulling at their synapses. Back to the crux of this book—what does this mean as more and more children are onboarding onto these platforms, even before they are technically supposed to be there, and what does this mean for us as parents?

CHAPTER SIX

THE AGE OF THE DIGITAL NATIVE

Dora the Explorer taught Kaylie her first swear word.

Kaylie was sitting on her favorite kitchen stool, head-phones on, watching YouTube cartoons. After the video ended, she walked over to me and said, "Hey, Dad, what does 'shit' mean?" (Note: the actual word was far worse, and I don't want to repeat it here).

My mouth dropped open. "What?? Where did you learn that word?"

"Oh, I just heard it on this video." I immediately looked at what she had just watched and, sure enough, there was Dora the Explorer. Swearing like a sailor.

It wasn't the "real" Dora; some wisecrack had dubbed in all kinds of bad language over the original cartoon.

I was disgusted. *Why would someone do that?* My next thought was, *what is a video like this doing on YouTube?*

Over time, I've definitely learned that my experience was not unique. I recently came across a *New York Times* article in which parents described similar stories: their children had found inappropriate video segments doctored into cartoons, from Mickey Mouse to Paw Patrol.[1]

There was one notable difference between these parents' stories and mine. My daughter had been on YouTube. This article was describing videos on YouTube Kids.

YouTube Kids came out with the promise of being safer for children, but it hasn't consistently delivered. Part of this comes down to an issue with volume: while YouTube has hired a lot more people to review and moderate content, they simply can't keep up with the influx of videos to comb through.[2] An enormous amount of content is uploaded and made available to kids every day on both the YouTube and the YouTube Kids platforms (to the tune of 300 hours of video being uploaded to YouTube every minute!),[3] and we as parents have to take an active role in monitoring exposure.

We're letting our youngest generations explore the online

---

1   Sapna Maheshwari, "On YouTube Kids, Startling Videos Slip Past Filters," *New York Times*, November 4, 2017.

2   Sam Levin, "Google to Hire Thousands of Moderators after Outcry over YouTube Abuse Videos," *The Guardian,* December 5, 2017.

3   "YouTube by the Numbers," *Omnicore,* January 6, 2019.

world, and it's difficult to keep tabs on so much virtual activity, especially given the size of the menu available and younger demographics.

Even apps "designed for kids" are often retrofitted versions of adult apps (lookin' at you, YouTube Kids), or apps that contain the same feature sets as many social media platforms. This makes it difficult to determine whether all the content and features are truly age-appropriate. Many kids' social networks still encourage users to amass followers (remember PopJam?) and include mechanisms for social validation. Not to mention the younger users who are joining social media earlier than they're supposed to: the Terms of Use of most social media apps is 13 years old, but Common Sense Media reports that the average kid gets their first social media account at age 12.6,[4] while Influence Central estimates are even younger at age 11.4.[5] In either case, children are clearly getting onto social media before the Terms of Use say they can.[6] In fact, 50 percent of kids have social media accounts by age 12.[7] There is no denying that platforms including Snapchat, Instagram, YouTube, TikTok, and to a lesser degree Facebook have features that appeal to

4   Jacqueline Howard, "What's the Average Age When Kids Get a Social Media Account?" *CNN*, June 22, 2018.

5   "Kids & Tech: The Evolution of Today's Digital Natives," *Influence Central*, 2016.

6   Jacqueline Howard, "What's the Average Age When Kids Get a Social Media Account?" *CNN*, June 22, 2018.

7   "Kids & Tech: The Evolution of Today's Digital Natives," *Influence Central*, 2016.

children under the age of 13, and all of these platforms have a large number of users who aren't supposed to be there per their Terms of Use.

Despite its efforts to moderate content, Google is still having trouble patrolling its YouTube and YouTube Kids platforms—dubbed videos get past filters, and the risk of accessing overtly dangerous (sexual content, for example) and subtly damaging (violent material) content remains high.

HIDDEN CONTENT

In July 2018, a nine-year-old girl told her mother about something disturbing on YouTube. In the middle of a cartoon the young girl was watching, a man in sunglasses appeared, explaining to kids how to commit suicide by slitting their wrists.[8] The mother, Dr. Free N. Hess was of course mortified and contacted YouTube, which removed the video a week later. (It took a full week!)

When the suicide video cropped up again—this time on the standard version of YouTube, Dr. Hess, a Florida-based pediatrician, voiced her concern about the issue bluntly on her *PediMom* blog:

---

8   Doug Criss, "A Mom Found Videos on YouTube Kids That Gave Children Instructions for Suicide," *CNN*, February 25, 2019.

My research has led me into a horrifying world where people create cartoons glorifying dangerous topics and scenarios such as self-harm, suicide, sexual exploitation, trafficking, domestic violence, sexual abuse, and gun violence which includes a simulated school shooting. All of these videos were found on YouTube Kids, a platform that advertises itself to be a safe place for children 8 years old and under.[9]

This isn't supposed to happen with kid-centric apps, but these "oversights" prove that we can't rely on the platforms to police themselves for age-appropriate content. Further, the Children's Online Privacy Protection Act (COPPA) was instituted in 1998 to protect the interests and privacy of kids when online. Unfortunately, it is proving quite easy for the large platforms to skirt the COPPA rules by "ignoring" the fact that children are even on their platforms.

THE GRAY AREA OF COPPA

On March 30, 2019, Mark Zuckerberg of all people posted an op-ed in the *Washington Post* calling for more regulation in technology.[10] While his piece caused many eyes to roll given the role that Facebook has played in

---

9   Dr. Free N. Hess, "YouTube Kids. There Is Still a HUGE Problem," *PediMom* (blog), 2019.

10 Mark Zuckerberg, "Mark Zuckerberg: The Internet Needs New Rules. Let's Start in These Four Areas," *Washington Post,* March 30, 2019.

many transgressions of user data and privacy, I think his message is solid. We should place more of an emphasis on keeping platforms more private and free of harmful content.

However, his op-ed piece left out what I feel is a crucial and unaddressed aspect of the conversation—there is very little emphasis on young people despite all of the statistics (and the smell test) telling us that kids are on technology, and in massive numbers. The potential impact of technology on developing minds and largely unprepared users—kids under 13—is massive and deserves more attention from the tech community as well as regulators.

Though platforms with users under the age of 13 need to comply with the Federal Trade Commission's Children's Online Privacy and Protection Act (COPPA), most can still operate in a gray area by simply "ignoring" the fact that children are online. In reality, many still use a number of different strategies to market directly to this segment, and they've seen significant user growth as a result. Remember, at the end of the day, platforms derive a great deal of value from their user counts, so they are enjoying the benefits of the extra users being there.

COPPA was established in April 2000 by the Federal Trade Commission (FTC), and it maintains guidelines that protect children and their data when online. Any platform with users under the age of 13 in the US must adhere to COPPA's guidelines or face fines of $16,000 per affected child. Without getting into too much detail, COPPA regulations are very strict and have a significant impact on the design of any platform that anticipates, or markets to, users under 13. Similar restrictions exist under Europe's General Data Protection Regulation-Kids (GDPR-K). These rules are no joke. They make it difficult to develop platforms for kids—and that's a good thing. When kids are involved, we should be erring on the side of safety.

So, with the statistics presented earlier this chapter, we know that kids are using all sorts of platforms including YouTube, Snapchat, TikTok, Instagram, and Facebook. So those platforms must all comply with COPPA, right?

Guess again.

When large platforms are more interested in monthly active user counts than child safety, it's unfortunately all too easy for them to circumvent COPPA and GDPR-K altogether.

When kids under 13 sign up for accounts on large platforms (note that they do have to lie about their age and generally have to have an email address to complete sign-up), the platforms face a critical choice. When they acknowledge that kids under the age of 13 are on their platform, they need to put processes in place to ensure they comply with COPPA.

Alternatively, they can point to their Terms of Use, say their platforms are for ages 13+, and more or less ignore COPPA. That may work in theory, but we know that kids are using the platforms and the stats back it up. But again Facebook, Instagram, YouTube, Snapchat, and TikTok all derive a great deal of their value from their user counts, so implementing COPPA-compliant flows would not only be extremely costly, but it would impact a very important metric for them by cutting out a significant segment.

Because of their Terms of Use, social media, gaming, and content sites can operate outside of COPPA, which doesn't require nearly as much parental control, verification, monitoring, and reporting. The platforms get to capitalize on the fact that children under 13 are included in their monthly user counts—and they benefit from the improved metrics, higher valuations, and increased ad dollars that come with it.

Meanwhile, children are able to connect with strangers, share personal information, and become targets for advertising algorithms. The underage audience is exposed to adult features like comment boards (which can be extremely toxic places) and thrust prematurely into a world of comparison and validation, and in-app tracking.

It is unfair to place the onus of protection squarely on parents, but that is unfortunately the reality today, and it won't change until regulators step in and take action to eliminate this gray area, and do it in a big way. Recently, TikTok was hit with a record $5.7 million fine from the FTC because they were collecting personal information from children under the age of 13.[11] Though it seems like a large sum, the amount is a drop in the bucket for TikTok's parent company, ByteDance, that's worth an estimated $75 billion. When a fine is only 0.007 percent of the company's value, it's hardly enough to be a real deterrent. We'll need to see much larger fines before any of the platforms make changes. As with Facebook earlier, I'd argue that companies will trade the minuscule fine for additional users anytime.

---

11   Sherisse Pham, "TikTok Hit with Record Fine for Collecting Data on Children," *CNN Business,* February 28, 2019.

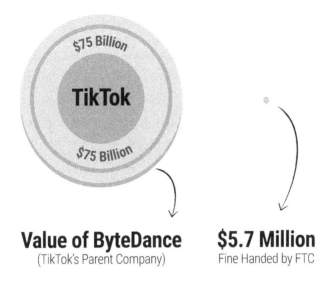

Value of ByteDance
(TikTok's Parent Company)

$5.7 Million
Fine Handed by FTC

It is encouraging that advertisers sometimes intervene when platforms won't; YouTube recently disabled comments on videos that feature children after many predatory comments were appearing.[12] However, they only took the action after major advertisers including Disney, Epic Games, and Nestle threatened to walk. While this was a positive development, things like this will always be reactive in nature, after safety has somehow been compromised.

For now though, it is largely up to us parents to help our kids explore this new world.

---

12 Julia Alexander, "YouTube is Disabling Comments on Almost All Videos Featuring Children," *The Verge*, February 28, 2019.

IT'S A WHOLE NEW WORLD

Prior to writing this book, if you asked me what brand I thought was most popular among children, I would have guessed names like Disney, LEGO, Barbie, or the current flavor-of-the-month fad like fidget spinners. Up until a few years ago, I might have been right.

It's much different today. Youth and family research firm Smarty Pants conducted a Brand Love Study in 2018 and found the most popular brand among US kids ages 6 to 12 is YouTube.[13] The rest of the top ten is equally telling:

2. Netflix
3. iPhone
4. McDonald's
5. Oreo
6. M&M's
7. Doritos
8. iPad
9. Xbox
10. Google

Other names from the study stood out as well, like Fortnite (11), Playstation (15), Instagram (27), Snapchat (28), Minecraft (38), Amazon (40), YouTube Kids (45), and Roblox (46). Maybe I'm showing my age, but I was

---

13 Jeremy Dickson, "Study: SVOD & Video App Brands Most Popular with Kids," *Kidscreen*, July 19, 2018.

very surprised to see Google more popular than Disney (19) and LEGO (22). It's fascinating how "old standby" engagement vehicles for kids have tumbled so far down the list, and it reiterates we are in a digital age. Kids are using this stuff, they know all about it, and they're not waiting until they're older to dive in.

Social media consumes kids today as well, as on average they score their first social media accounts sometime between the ages of 11.4 and 12.6, as mentioned earlier. The largest percentage of kids, at 39 percent, get their first social media account between ages 10 and 12, but another 11 percent signed on when they were *younger than 10*.[14]

As of August 2017, Statista shows 23.5 million kids age 11 and under on Snapchat, 14.5 million on Instagram, and 3.1 million on Facebook.[15] I can also only imagine how many of YouTube's 1.9 billion monthly active users are under the age of 13—looking at all the kids on the platform around my household or any public area, I'm guessing it is extremely significant.

14   "Kids & Tech: The Evolution of Today's Digital Natives," *Influence Central*, 2016.

15   "Number of Child, Teen, and Young Adult Facebook, Instagram, and Snapchat Users in the United States as of August 2017 (in Millions)," *Statista*, 2017.

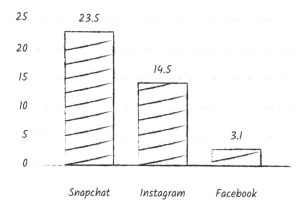

Number of kids age 11 and under on social media platforms in US as of August 2017 (in millions)

Snapchat — 23.5
Instagram — 14.5
Facebook — 3.1

Meanwhile, there is an entire industry growing around the live streaming of video games. Twitch Interactive, a subsidiary of Amazon, is leading the way, with more than 15 million daily active users. As with leading social media sites, Twitch's Terms of Use state users must be 13 or older. There's no doubt that kids are skirting the rules and using Twitch. There are also countless You-Tube channels featuring videos that are narrated by the video creator as they play popular games like Minecraft or Roblox. These are all examples of content that definitely appeal to children but are hosted by platforms that technically don't allow them.

As a parent, this information has naturally given me a lot to consider and keep an eye on. Kaylie is eight now, and it's likely that she will soon want an age-restricted social media account. One of her friends, whose parents are a little more liberal with this trend, got on to TikTok. I later checked it out when Kaylie asked if she could use it; it looked like a fun app at first. But quickly after opening the app, a girl in a bikini popped on the screen, busting out all kinds of racy moves while lip-syncing to a song. It was easy to say no to that one.

DESIGN FLAWS AND DESIGN FEATURES

The apps and platforms that I've discussed at length in this book were never designed with kids in mind. Even platforms like YouTube Kids are retrofitted products, and still feature many of the "sticky" features of its parent apps. But our kids look up to their parents and want to be like them (go figure). Children are extremely observant, and modern parents must be very vigilant about their own habits and behaviors. For example, I have a two-year-old son who works his way to the TV and tries to swipe it—because that's how he sees mom and dad interact with media. If your child sees you interacting with your phone all day and swiping through Instagram or Facebook feeds, it's only natural that they may want that experience too.

Some apps for kids do seem to be trying to do right by kids and parents. Facebook Messenger for Kids, for example, doesn't use ads or vanity metrics features that could be concerning to parents—but the ultimate goal is still to convert those children into adult users when the time comes. Also, I'd be giving Facebook even more information on myself if I were to use Messenger with my kids. Facebook would then know I am a father of two, have the full names of my children, and could potentially glean other data about them including gender, birthday, and age (I have to optionally share some of this with them). I'm sure that would increase the likelihood I'd start seeing ads for age- and gender-appropriate toys, games, and products in my Facebook feed if I were to use Messenger with my kids.

Other kid-centric apps, like PopJam, are developed specifically for kids—but include problematic features such as "likes" and followers that fuel social validation.

We also have to be critical about what behaviors are being encouraged with certain app usage. In an interview, the founder of TikTok described how he made it compulsory for all management team members to make their own TikTok videos—and if they didn't get a certain number of "likes," they had to do a bunch of push-ups.[16] It's a rudimentary motivation, sure. An exercise like this signals the kind of culture, values, and metrics the company ultimately wants to pass on to its user base.

---

16 Julia Glum, "Meet the Head of TikTok, a 35-Year-Old Who Makes Employees Do Pushups If They Don't Get Enough Likes," *Yahoo Finance,* January 10, 2019.

In that regard, I valiantly try to directly engage with my daughter's online activity. She currently has a Roblox account, which has an age limit of 12 and up. I let her engage with this particular app because it has several good features: you can build stuff and use problem-solving skills, and I can take an active role when she's using it. She's also a big Minecraft fan, and we started doing a coding class together so she can do her own mods. As she explores these apps, she's learning and getting an appreciation for how they work. I'm learning alongside her and increasing my comfort level at the same time.

Exploring apps together creates a way for me to manage her activity and assess whether I'm going to let her on platforms with a little gray area in them. Again, this speaks to my responsibility as a parent to be actively engaged as I navigate new technologies with my daughter.

THE RISE OF KID TECH

In addition to kids moving onto adult platforms, a new market is emerging known as kid tech. While it is encouraging that products entering this segment are generally COPPA-compliant and feature more control for parents, my concern is that many products have simply decided to build a child version of the most popular adult apps. In other words, there are too many products that basically label themselves as "like Instagram, but for kids."

The issue with this is that these platforms contain much of the same features, including "likes," comments, and followers, that are used to keep users coming back to the platform.

I worry that as these apps are moving into spaces with younger users, we see lots of evidence of learned behavior. My daughter, for example, is very interested in Snapchat filters and doing goofy faces with cat ears and that sort of thing. When she's done with the photo, however, she has no real need or even desire to share it with everyone. She's content simply interacting with the technology. With age comes the natural gravitation toward more social interaction, but app companies are still intent on moving that life stage into younger demographics and introducing features that subsequently lead to social validation issues.

For example, when Kaylie posts her online artwork and apps like PopJam start introducing "likes," the chemical dopamine cycle kicks in and trains her that those kinds of things are important. Suddenly she begins caring about followers and the popularity of other posts she makes. While we know we crave social validation from others, I don't believe that children intuitively crave these interactions from tech. But as we've learned, apps that promote these types of features are taking advantage of our human needs and brain chemicals to introduce them to obsessive elements that can be problematic.

Fortunately, the child segment has rejected many of the apps that have tried to move into the space with social media-types of features. A recent Tech and Play study gauged children's interest levels in different categories of apps. Unsurprisingly, video was very strong, with more than 75 percent of users, while just 40 percent favored social networking.[17] Kids were much more interested in things like video chat, reading, education, and games; the study validated what we see in the market.

That's a good thing, as a recent study that we'll detail below showed that while it may not be natural for kids to crave "likes" and social validation from tech, when they are exposed to these features, they can become very meaningful for children, very quickly.

A LIFE IN "LIKES"

As we teach our children how to engage in the digital age, it's not just the safety of content or the appropriateness of particular features we have to watch out for. As our children grow into tech, they're also growing into their identities and sense of self-worth.

I guess it's nothing new for sage advice from elders to fall on deaf ears of young people, but today it includes bat-

---

17   "Exploring Play and Creativity in Pre-Schoolers' Use of Apps," *Tech and Play,* 2019.

tling with invisible foes: modern-day kids face significant pressure to be like the online Joneses.

A UK-based study unveiled a great many concerning stats and findings. In the study "Life in 'Likes': Children's Commissioner Report into Social Media Use among 8–12 year olds," children described how they felt as they built profiles and interacted with others online. The researchers noted that as children started to extend their network beyond their close family and friends, they also began to compare themselves more heavily to others on social media. When they started to follow celebrities, they "felt those comparisons were unattainable."[18]

"Despite talking about the importance of 'staying true to yourself' and being authentic on social media," the researchers wrote, "girls were worried about looking 'pretty' and boys were more concerned with looking 'cool' and having the right clothing."

"Will my picture get any 'likes?'"

"How do I look today?"

"Is this good enough to share?"

---

18   "Life in 'Likes': Children's Commissioner Report into Social Media Use among 8–12 Year Olds," *Children's Commissioner Report*, January 4, 2018.

"Children felt good when they got 'likes' and 'comments' from friends," the report noted, and some Year 7 children were starting to become dependent on them, using techniques to guarantee they would get a high number of 'likes.' Children started to see offline activities through a 'shareable lens' based on what would look best on social media." This is what I described earlier in this book with the notion of avatars, or online personas, that begin to deviate from who we really are.

This study reflects that we need to have open and honest conversations with our children about their experiences as they venture out into the digital world, so that we can understand how their interactions are shaping their sense of self.

Tech is here, and kids are on it. It's not a question of *if* we'll let them engage with it, but *how*. We as parents must ensure that we are facilitating the right structures (as described with the zoo metaphor I used earlier in this book), and asking the right questions. The common question I hear from parents—*how much screen time should I let my kid have?*—is actually the wrong question. In the next chapter, you'll see why—and we'll start asking the right questions about our kids' use of tech.

CHAPTER SEVEN

THE BRAVE NEW WORLD OF PARENTING

One day recently I noticed a mysterious $10 charge from my Apple ID. I didn't recognize the vendor name. I racked my memory to figure out where the expense had come from, and then I realized: the charge didn't come from me. It was a charge from Dash Tag, a game my daughter was playing.

I was livid.

She had pestered me regularly to download games for her, and I eventually relented and gave her my password—a mistake that, I later learned, I'm not alone in making as a parent (like I tell my kids though, that doesn't excuse it!). I trusted her, and the nature of the apps she was drawn to. I still do. But in giving her my password, I'd given her much more freedom than she proved she could handle.

In the Dash Tag game, players can acquire crystals which act as currency. They can use the crystals to buy things like costumes and upgrades for the characters. Kaylie had made an in-app purchase on her own.

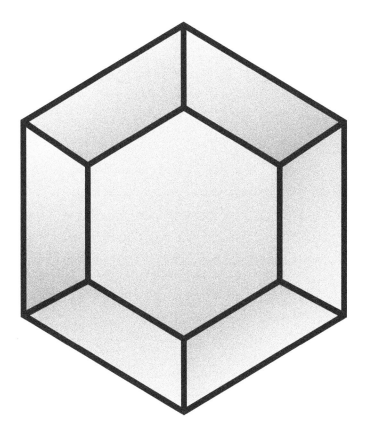

I hit the roof when that charge came through. We had a long conversation about it. I told her that what she'd done equated to stealing. We talked about what it means to breach trust, and how long it takes to rebuild once you break it. She lost the use of the iPad for a while, and now I'm the gatekeeper for everything she wants to do through the App Store.

About a week later, I found out her decision stemmed from (shockingly) peer pressure. Kaylie's friends had made similar purchases, and she was falling behind in the game in terms of crystals and rewards. Pressure from friends, whether real or perceived, prompted her to make the decision when she knew it was wrong.

SCREEN TIME VS. SCREEN CAPTURED

When I speak with parents and attend industry events, the first question I'm asked from parents (once they know what I do) is "how much screen time should we allow?" I know they mean well, but I tell them that they are asking the wrong question. What I tell them instead is that rather than focusing on the time spent on screens, they need to look at what their children are *doing* on those screens.

Don't get me wrong—we have limits on screen time in my household. For the record, Kaylie currently gets 30 minutes on weekdays, 45 minutes on the weekdays that she has karate class, and 2 hours on weekends. But those limits aren't in place because I think something magical happens in her brain after one of the rather arbitrary time limits. Instead, those are the quantities of time that my wife and I are comfortable with, where we feel that Kaylie is getting a good balance of activities.

You see, screen time alone isn't the enemy; as with many things in life, quality is much more important than quantity. And not all screen time is created equal.

As Jaron Lanier pointed out in the interview "How Social Media Ruins Your Life," there is a difference between *screen* time and *manipulation* time.

Lanier, a pioneer in virtual reality and outspoken critic of all things social media, described how in our time spent online, we're experiencing a mild version of behavioral modification all the time. For kids in particular, the time they spend "being observed by algorithms and tweaked by them is vastly worse than screen time itself."[1] Manipulation time, Lanier contends, inevitably leads to negative outcomes.

There's a distinction, he says, between manipulation and addiction. We've already discussed the ramifications of the dopamine cycle to keep users engaged in a particular app, and the extent to which social media platforms

1   "Jaron Lanier Interview on How Social Media Ruins Your Life," YouTube video, posted by *Channel 4 News*, June 15, 2018.

use engagement to, in essence, force addictive behavior. Manipulation, however, is different: it influences the user to take action, whether it's buying a product, voting for a certain person in an election, or responding in a certain way to a news story.

When algorithms, apps, and platforms are driving our behavior, we can become "screen captured." As we become aware of how these mechanisms are working in the background to keep us online, we'll be better able to pull ourselves out of those cycles when it's not what we intend.

BEING SCREEN CAPTURED

Now that I've given a lot of background into how platforms attract and retain our information, how advertisers and other third parties use data that is collected, and introduced the term "screen captured," let's look into some specific examples that you can watch out for as a parent.

RABBIT HOLES

The most prevalent form of screen capture in my household comes from YouTube. I (and I'm sure others) call this the "YouTube rabbit hole." YouTube continuously serves up recommended videos on auto-play, with the goal of keeping users on the platform so they can serve up the next ad at the beginning or middle of the next video. Subscription on-demand video services like Netflix also have auto-play features, and they'll play episode after episode if you let them. Netflix may not feature ads, but this is very intentional in keeping its platform more "sticky."

We've established channels and playlists that are safe and appropriate for my daughter and try to keep her on them as much as possible. We talk to her about what happens when she clicks a recommended video in the "Up Next" menu on YouTube, and how far that can take her from what she intended to watch. We also have her turn off the auto-play features so that she has to consciously make a choice to click on the next video. Understanding that these features on YouTube and Netflix are there intentionally to keep us (and our kids) on the platform longer and turning them off is a good first step in shifting the balance away from manipulative time.

THE ALGORITHMS THINK YOU'LL LIKE THIS

I've previously talked about the fact that algorithms themselves alone aren't the enemy, but they are definitely designed to attract and retain our attention. We have to be aware of this fact as parents when our kids are exposed to them.

I think we need to steer our kids away from platforms with algorithmically curated feeds—including Facebook, Instagram, Twitter, and Snapchat—at least without close supervision. Parents are also well-advised to heed the 13+ age limit in the Terms of Service. I have to admit that this is very easy for me to say with an eight- and two-year-old right now, and it is possible that my stance may change as my children age. That said, if I decide to let them onto one of these platforms, there will be rules in place to ensure that I have visibility into what they are doing.

YouTube deserves special attention here because, as discussed, it's the most popular platform among kids aged 6 to 12. While it doesn't have a "feed" per se, it still operates with algorithms designed to pull us in. Since I've already shared how my daughter enjoys the platform, I'm not going to tell you to ban it for your kids. I'll just warn you that the recommended videos can again draw your kids into the proverbial rabbit hole. The way it works is by analyzing our viewing history and suggesting similar content. But remember, YouTube doesn't just do this to keep you endlessly entertained. They do it to keep you screen captured and show you as many ads as possible in the process.

The danger of the manipulation is not just in the advertisements. One recent study found that toddlers have a 45 percent chance of clicking through to inappropriate content within just ten recommended videos.[2] The authors of the study identified the "dangers of crowd-sourced, uncurated content combined with engagement-oriented, gameable recommendation systems," and I have to say I share their concerns, especially when family members are sharing a device or account. When the algorithm can't distinguish between users, recommendations get jumbled together, and your toddler might see suggestions based on your teenager's recent views.

Algorithms can screen capture you by serving you content you like. But there's arguably an even greater danger when you're on a platform that uses social validation to show you exactly how many people *like you*.

SOCIAL VALIDATION AND COMPARISON

Vanity metrics are ubiquitous across platforms, and they lead to screen capture by giving us a sense of social valida-

---

2   Konstantinos Papadamou, "Disturbed YouTube for Kids: Characterizing and Detecting Inappropriate Videos Targeting Young Children," *arXive.org,* January 21, 2019.

tion. As discussed, "likes" and follower counts—among other metrics—are known to trigger dopamine in our brain the same way gambling does. We anticipate a reward when we post on a social channel, and it's no accident that tech companies exploit this human drive to feel accepted. It's an intentional strategy to hook you in, and the platforms reap the benefit of increased daily and monthly active users who become obsessed with those metrics.

Companies have leveraged the dopamine reward cycle as well as FOMO (Fear of Missing Out, which is driven by our desire for belonging and acceptance) to keep us highly engaged with their platforms. The same will hold true for our children if they are exposed to the same features. The jury may be out on exactly how impactful social validation is on the psyche and how much it is tied to the recent spikes in anxiety and depressive symptoms, but it is a risk I want to avoid for my children and why I've steered my daughter away from platforms that feature these vanity metrics.

KIDFLUENCERS

YouTube's top-grossing channel in 2018 was started by a seven-year-old boy named Ryan who does toy reviews. Ryan earned about $22 million from this channel in 2018, signaling a growing new phenomenon: "kidfluencers."

Ryan's success at marketing to kids on YouTube is a startling example of manipulation—this time specifically directed at children. "Unboxing videos" are common on YouTube, and are highly appealing to children who, ironically, are not supposed to be on the platform in the first place.

After his success on YouTube, Ryan partnered with a company named Pocket.Watch that helps kidfluencers with sizable followings build their YouTube channels into fully fledged brands. In the past year, Ryan has put out his own line of toys marketed by Pocket.Watch. He's also featured in a video game that uses his likeness: "Tag with Ryan." I was recently in New York City and visited Times Square. Among all the bright lights was a billboard featuring Ryan for his new feature series on Nickelodeon.

The problem to me with this type of content is that it isn't always clear that it is, for all intents and purposes, an ad. Influencer marketing as a whole has been under a lot of scrutiny lately on all platforms, most notably Instagram, and rules and guidelines aren't always followed when it comes to identifying the content as a paid ad. That being said, I think most adults are aware of the fact that when an influential figure promotes a product or brand, they are very likely being compensated in some way.

I don't think kids can make that same distinction. Fortunately, my daughter hasn't shown much interest in these types of videos. If she was more interested, I'd try my best to have her watch other things, but would definitely make the point of explaining to her how influencer marketing works.

ARBITRARY GOALS AND METRICS

Many apps and platforms use arbitrary goals and metrics to screen capture. I've previously discussed a few examples earlier in this book.

Snapstreaks are a good example of how a platform uses goals and metrics to drive behavior. In the case of Snapchat, they want you (and at least one of your friends) engaging with the platform every single day. For what? To keep an arbitrary streak alive. This is where goals and metrics can hook us in. Sometimes this can be positive; for instance, we may want to keep a streak of days going to the gym intact. In the case of the platforms, it is so you will continue to count as a daily or monthly active user.

The Snapchat score—the counter, discussed earlier in the book, that accumulates with every post shared or received—is another example. Others include arbitrary follower counts, numbers of "likes," features that unlock when a certain number of followers is reached, and the number of "friends" that we have on a platform.

The issue with these metrics is that, as we've seen earlier in the book, we (and our kids) will sometimes go to unhealthy lengths to achieve these goals or metrics. The kid who shares their password while on vacation to keep their Snapstreak alive and the 13-year-old who felt the need to rack up a thousand Snapchat points are only a few examples.

IN-APP PURCHASES

Young users are particularly vulnerable to manipulation, and privacy and children's organizations are taking notice. In early 2019, a coalition of these organizations filed a Federal Trade Commission (FTC) complaint against Facebook for its structure for in-app purchases in games. Children are able to make these purchases without parental permission, the group argued, and young users may not be aware that some items cost money.[3]

In fact, some active young users who make a lot of in-app purchases on their parents' accounts are sometimes referred to as "whales"—a term inspired by gambling culture that refers to the high rollers who essentially fund casinos with their losses.

Social media and app companies use it to describe

---

3   Danielle Abril, "Facebook Once Again Under Fire for In-App Purchases Made by Children," *Fortune*, February 21, 2019.

children and teenagers who make lots of app-related purchases. A *New York Times* article described the phenomenon: "Many mobile games have features that lure children into making in-app purchases using their parents' credit cards while playing; it has become so prevalent that a new term was coined, 'bait apps,' which have been featured in class-action lawsuits."[4]

Bait apps make it extremely easy to make additional purchases by linking add-ons to existing accounts and associated payment engines. They make it a breeze for children to get on a platform and experience it, but then tease users with additional goodies that they can't have for free. They turn screen-captured kids into customers.

This, of course, is a big deal. In 2014, the Federal Trade Commission forced Apple to issue more than $32.5 million in refunds to customers whose children made purchases through the App Store without parental consent.[5]

Also in 2014, Google paid out at least $19 million for the same reason through the Play Store.[6] In 2017, the FTC

---

4   Brian X. Chen, "Are Your Children Racking Up Charges from Mobile Games?" *New York Times,* February 6, 2019.

5   Edward Wyatt and Brian X. Chen, "Apple to Refund App Store Purchases Made Without Parental Consent," *New York Times,* January 15, 2014.

6   "Google to Refund Consumers at Least $19 Million to Settle FTC Complaint It Unlawfully Billed Parents for Children's Unauthorized In-App Charges," *Federal Trade Commission,* September 4, 2014.

made a similar deal with Amazon for in-app purchases; more than $70 million of purchases may be eligible for refunds.[7]

What I find especially troubling is the platforms are very aware of what they're doing: for each of these platforms, internal teams are tasked to create programs specifically to entice additional purchases. While I don't excuse Kaylie's (or my own) behavior, I understand how she was funneled into it. Children and younger teens are impressionable and easily influenced, and on the other side of their games are developers who are very motivated to influence them to do specific things. Combine paywalls in games with pressure from friends, and it's easy to see how difficult these decisions are for young minds to make.

POSITIVE SCREEN TIME

The last thing I want to do is encourage technophobia. In fact, I'm a firm believer that technology can have a positive impact on us and our kids. Just think about the incredible amount of information that kids have access to—literally at their fingertips. When used responsibly, technology can open up minds and introduce adventure.

Growing up pre-internet, this kind of access to knowledge

---

7   "Refunds Now Available from Amazon for Unauthorized In-App Purchases," *Federal Trade Commission*, May 30, 2017.

is something I couldn't have imagined in my youth. I was limited to what I could find at the local library or in my parent's encyclopedia set. I still remember the day that we got our first CD-ROM encyclopedia, which seems quaint now, but was nothing short of mind-blowing at the time. As an eager student, I relied on this new technology to improve my school work. But the 700-megabyte capacity of a CD-ROM is nothing compared to the amount of information on the internet. Just between Google, Amazon, Microsoft, and Facebook servers, there is an estimated 1.2 million terabytes of data! This is many, many orders of magnitude more information than what I had access to as a kid—and when used responsibly, it's an invaluable resource for young learners.

I've witnessed firsthand how access to information can inspire kids. My daughter uses tech to learn about anything and everything on her mind, and I coach her on how to ask the right questions in search engines and identify reliable results. This week, she learned about birthstones (and she's concluded that my ruby is prettier than her opal). Under my supervision, she also plays games like Roblox and Minecraft—which help hone her problem-solving, creativity, and collaboration skills. She plays online with her friends and is banned from connecting with anyone we don't know personally. Together, she and her friends solve problems and have a lot of fun exploring.

And you can't talk about tech without talking about connection. My daughter is able to stay in touch with family and friends in a way that simply wasn't possible before the internet. When we moved to Vancouver in 2017, she had to leave friends behind. It used to be that, when a kid moved away, that was the last you saw of them. Today, my daughter uses FaceTime to talk to faraway friends and family—and we've even used tech to plan a sleepover with an old schoolmate that she hadn't physically seen in over a year when Kaylie visited her grandparents in Calgary (whom she also talks to regularly over FaceTime).

Kaylie has also taken quite the liking to reading books online. We subscribe to a great app called Epic! which gives her access to tens of thousands of books. She is about to finish her grade 3 year, and to date, Kaylie has read 1,112 books, turned more than 71 thousand pages, and spent 217 hours reading (this doesn't count toward her time limit).

Finally, screens can provide endless entertainment. Sure, I had TV when I was young, but there were only a few hours each day of child-friendly programming. Thanks to Netflix, YouTube, and on-demand TV, there's always something entertaining and appropriate for my daughter to enjoy (as long as I'm actively vetting things). We watch a lot of shows together, and she spends a lot of time on the YouTube channels I've pre-approved. I'll also admit that my wife and I occasionally put my two-year-old son in front of *Baby Shark*, because he loves it and it gives us a small break. But we are incredibly mindful of not falling into the rabbit hole and have turned off auto-play. I have also subscribed to YouTube Premium, which is ad-free. With as much as we use it in our household, I made the conscious decision to pay for the platform in another currency than ourselves (for the advertisers). It doesn't eliminate all of the manipulative features and risks of the platform, but it definitely helps.

These are just a few examples of how screen time has had a positive impact on my family. With proper supervision, the wealth of information on the internet can help kids learn. Games can encourage skill development. Devices can solidify connections with loved ones. And of course, Baby Shark can induce giggles. There is a big difference, though, between our kids enjoying screen time, and our kids becoming screen captured.

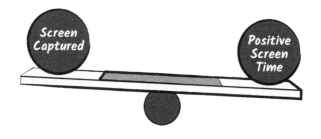

Screen Captured
· Rabbit Holes
· Algorithms
· Social Validation and Comparison
· Kidfluencers
· Arbitrary Goals and Metrics
· Sneaky In-App Purchases

Positive Screen Time
· Access to Information
· Learning
· Problem Solving
· Creativity
· Collaboration
· Connection
· Reading
· Monitored Entertainment

This is why I make the distinction between the two and steer parents away from the "time on screens" question. I'd much rather my daughter spend two hours reading books or talking with her grandparents online than even 10 minutes chasing "likes" or followers.

Again, it is quality over quantity.

RESPONSIBLE OVERSIGHT IN THE DIGITAL AGE

Parents have a lot of responsibility in monitoring their children's online activity. Even if you want to follow the Terms of Use and wait until your child is 13 to sign them up for apps, educating them and mentoring them through that choice is still your responsibility. Certainly, if you're allowing them onto apps that aren't designed specifically for kids, it's even more crucial to help them navigate their activities safely. You can't expect media companies—that are in the business of making money by attracting users on their platform—to handle the parenting, too.

As we see in the example of YouTube Kids, the sheer volume of content uploaded every minute of every single day is astounding; there's just no way to field a large-enough staff to see everything. Much work is being done with artificial intelligence and other machine learning to better recognize and filter malicious content and delete fake accounts. However, even with these additional measures being implemented and improved, we will still have to keep a critical eye—even on kid-friendly apps.

It's not easy, though, when 80 percent of online videos are watched with the sound off or when your kids are camped out on the couch with headphones on, completely tuned out to everything else. Beyond vetting safe content for our kids, we also have to have conversations that make them feel comfortable to tell us when they've come across inappropriate content. In our house, I've focused on making sure that if my daughter does see something bad, she feels safe and comfortable telling me about it.

If a child sees something they shouldn't, a parent's first instinct might be to ban that platform or ban the device—

but I think that inevitably leads to the child covering up bad stuff next time and simply not telling her parents about it at all.

The most important thing to me is creating a safe culture and open dialogue. It's really the only way, with any measure of confidence, to keep on top of things. Many 11-year-old kids are in their rooms at night with the lights off, on their phones looking at who knows what. Comment boards under YouTube videos, for example, can be notoriously awful places. Even if a video is "appropriate," is the context still malicious? People often treat each other terribly online, and inappropriate content is out there all the time. The other important aspect, of course, is something we discussed earlier in the book—the platforms are always actively tracking information about your kid. If this is a concern to a parent, my recommendation is to keep the bedroom a device-free zone at night.

GUIDING OUR DIGITAL NATIVES TO HEALTHY HABITS

Short of unplugging everything and moving to a wooden shack in the middle of the Alaskan wilderness, what's a parent to do? The jury is still out on the ultimate effects of children engaging with social media at such early ages, but regardless of which side of the issue you're on, you have critical decisions to make as a parent about how to introduce your children to the online world.

My two-year-old son is currently watching YouTube videos of his favorite songs. It's easy to choose the content that he watches in these early years. It won't be long, though, before he's exploring the online world—as Kaylie is now. As children begin to navigate themselves and search on their own (and follow recommended videos in the YouTube rabbit hole), the job description for parents switches from providing the child's content to preparing them to take an active role on their own online journey.

While it's impossible to police every piece of online content, there are things we can do to help our children develop healthy social media habits. Once you've made the decision to introduce your child to technology, the best you can do as a parent is start early and be responsible with the content available to them.

While there are no hard-and-fast guidelines about what may or may not be appropriate for your individual child, there are certainly some general guidelines that I've found helpful to follow as I watch my own children branch out in the tech world.

SCREEN TIME VS. REAL TIME

Dr. Renae Beaumont points out that it's important to be mindful of how your children are spending their time, on screens and off. When their time is dominated by screens, children may be missing out on other important activities in their lives. "Activities that often get sacrificed for screen time include schoolwork, recreational reading, creative activities, physical activity, sleep and time spent informally hanging out with siblings or peers. All of these activities play a critical role in children developing the skills they need to achieve their potential in adulthood."[8]

Dr. Beaumont also recommends that screen time be used to engage with educational content, connect with family and friends, and create new content. As children engage with new apps, she echoes Jaron Lanier's concerns: it's important to pay attention to whether they're being shown ads, and to help them become aware of how apps are manipulating them into making purchases.

CREATION VERSUS CONSUMPTION

Dr. Beaumont touched on another critical element that I consider with my kid's tech use. In addition to tech itself being in proper balance with other activities, I try to make sure that my daughter has a good balance of creation versus consumption when on tech. Creation may involve taking and sharing pictures and videos privately with family, drawing or coloring on any one of many available apps, or building worlds in Minecraft or Roblox. The creative aspect is why we've decided to let Kaylie use

---

8   Dr. Renae Beaumont, personal email communication with the author, March 17, 2019.

Roblox despite being below the age threshold of 12+ on the App Store. I just make sure I have regular discussions with her about how she's using it and to make sure she's not connecting with strangers.

She watches her fair share of YouTube too. I think the sight of coming home to her sitting on the couch, mouth open, watching endless clips on YouTube happened one too many times. I've since thought about how to keep the balance of creation and consumption in check.

LOOK FOR "DIGITAL ON-RAMPS"

Diana Graber, an expert on digital literacy and the founder of Cyber Civics and Cyberwise, authored a fantastic book on the subject of kids and technology: *Raising Humans in a Digital World* (another must-read for parents in my view). In the book, Graber introduces a term, "digital on-ramps," which I think perfectly describes what I'm trying to do with my children. The book quotes Patti Connolly, longtime Waldorf educator, who says: "There are too many positive uses of screens today not to look for healthy ways to introduce their use to young children."[9] I couldn't agree more.

Graber then describes the term "digital on-ramps" in this context: "Just as a freeway on-ramp provides a safe way

---

9 Diana Graber, *Raising Humans in a Digital World* (New York: Amacom, 2019).

for a vehicle to accelerate to the speed of fast-moving traffic, a digital on-ramp offers the same approach to the information superhighway." She then provides some great examples of these on-ramps, such as video conferencing with loved ones, co-viewing educational content, writing emails together to friends and family, sending texts and pictures to relatives, playing family-friendly video games, and doing research.

Graber concludes that "a focus on the positive uses of tech—using it to connect with loved ones, to learn new things, to be creative—breeds positive online habits that will, hopefully, last a lifetime." Some of the ways I'm using technology with Kaylie definitely fit into the categories Graber describes, and I've found it incredibly positive.

CHECK YOUR OWN HABITS

Take care to watch your own behavior online. We're constantly modeling our own tech habits to our children, and it's not uncommon for us to be hypocritical. I can't tell you how many times I've seen a parent admonish a child for an online behavior, banish their child from tech, and then turn back to their own Instagram feed. Many parents (and adults in general) are just as obsessed with tech as kids are. If children only observe you staring at your phone, it's inevitable they'll want to do what you do, and they'll ask to be on the platforms you're on.

MONITOR HEADPHONE USE

Remember that Dora the Explorer video Kaylie found, where Dora swore like a sailor? I didn't immediately know Kaylie stumbled on that until she told me—because she was wearing headphones. Visually, a lot of content can look okay, but there could be more going on, literally, than meets the eye. It's important for parents to actually listen to what's being said in their children's content, and be conscious of what kinds of content they're letting their children listen to unsupervised.

HEAR THEM OUT

I've had a lot of time to reflect on the few instances that Kaylie has run into things online that concerned me: dubbed swear words, nasty comment threads, and vanity metrics come to mind first and foremost. It's important to be mindful of your own reaction when your child reports seeing something bad online. Often a parent's initial reaction is to say, "You're not going to be on You-Tube anymore." But I think in a case like that, what you're actually training is for your child not to report the next time they see something you'll disapprove of, whether on that platform or another. When banishment is the outcome of reporting, they'll be much less likely to report. If your child comes to you with examples of inappropriate content or conduct that they experienced online, it's important to positively reinforce their reporting. You can open up a broader discussion in terms of what that content means in the context of the platform they were on.

TAKE A TEST-DRIVE

There are plenty of resources available, led by Common Sense Media (commonsensemedia.org), for parents to do background checks on apps, including articles from specific organizations or study results outlining reasons why a specific game or app is okay or why not. I encourage parents to read up on the latest news anytime they are contemplating turning their child loose on a platform, but I think the best way is to test-drive an app first—and let your child do the driving.

In the five- to eight-year-old age range, kids are often starting to explore on their own and establish social circles, but family is still central. My daughter loves to share what she's doing with me and is excited to take me through her favorite games, so some of her screen time is time that we can spend together. Any time together is good time, and in the online realm there is no substitute for your child taking you through a game and telling you all about it. Along the way, you get a sense of the community and appreciate the platform for what it is and what it means in your child's life.

As you assess each app, here are some questions to help guide you:

- Look at the size of the community they're engaging. Can they connect only with friends, or with others in a bigger circle?
- How do they connect to others?
- Can parents have visibility into what's going on? How can parents intervene?
- What kinds of interactions can users have with people on the app?
- How easy is it for kids to disclose personal information?
- Are users being exposed to manipulative elements, such as algorithmically driven ads and in-app purchases that aren't always clear?
- Is currency used in some way, like in a game?
- Does the community have elements of social validation, such as "likes," followers, and commenting features?

As you explore and assess these features with your child, have conversations about what you find. Let them know which behaviors and content aren't safe or appropriate. Help them understand the impacts of their social interactions. Leave the door open for them to tell you when they've come across something that makes them uncomfortable. Keeping an open and ongoing dialogue will help you prepare your kids for increased freedom as they age.

AGE-APPROPRIATE CONVERSATIONS

Children will naturally be interested in different kinds of content at different ages, and each stage comes with its own challenges. Obviously, I'm not having many conversations with my infant son about online safety; he's not clicking around on the internet yet. But I'm certainly having those conversations with my eight-year-old. And down the road, when my children are in their tweens and teens, they'll naturally get more into social media, and be susceptible to social comparison. They'll likely value "likes" and followers alongside their peers—and we'll have very different conversations about that in the future than we're having about what they're exploring now.

And frankly, that's not a conversation I want to wait to have with Kaylie until she's 13. I remember when I was 13 and refused to heed any of my parents' advice. But by beginning conversations about tech now, at these earlier years, we have time to discuss our ideas about what is valuable in technology and what isn't.

Back when I found Kaylie on PopJam and became concerned at the features she was using, we talked at length about why I didn't want her on the app. We've already had discussions about what Facebook, Snapchat, and other social media introduce into her life. I'm laying a good groundwork now, so that we don't have these conversations for the first time when she's 13 or 14 and struggling to understand the online world she's stepping into.

Let's take a closer look at what each age range means, generally, for a child's development, and what they and their peers tend to explore.

AGES 4–5

Up to this age, a child's exposure to the internet might be limited to the YouTube content their parent puts in front of them. By four or five, kids are starting to click around, and it's important to start age-appropriate conversations.

Remember that as a child accesses any kind of platform, they're connecting to a whole online world, and they're also being exposed to a mass audience. They may be seeing the comment threads below YouTube videos, or even interacting with people in games. It's tempting as a parent to pick an age-appropriate app that moderates content, but you can't completely outsource the responsibility to review what your child is exposed to. Remember the YouTube Kids examples we highlighted at the top of this chapter: there's simply too much content for companies to reliably moderate.

Keep in mind features like auto-play that may expose your child to unexpected content or ads. For that reason,

Netflix is often a better choice than YouTube: the algorithms still cue up recommended content, but it's more likely to be consistently in the children's category, and it doesn't have ads. Be mindful of when your child is watching videos with headphones, as this may prevent you from knowing what content they're watching.

AGES 6–8

I think letting children explore on their own a little bit is great for confidence, curiosity, and creativity. As you decide to let your child expand their online activity, be prepared to guide them closely to moderate content and help them understand what they're accessing. Watch out for features that encourage social validation and vanity metrics, as well as manipulation tactics in the form of ads and in-app purchases.

Don't make the same mistake I made; keep sole control of your password. You need to vet any apps your child wants to try, and have to be aware of any purchases they want to make. Any app with an in-app purchase is going to be tied to an existing account with automatic payments. Behind all of that is a password, and giving your kids access to that opens up more possibilities than just downloading apps. It can be a headache to evaluate every new app, but giving the responsibility of a password to a child too soon means trouble (as I learned the hard way).

As they get on new platforms and games, have your child give you a test-drive through each app they want to use, and ask them about what features they like and why. If you decide not to let your child use an app they've expressed an interest in, explain why. Point out the features that are problematic (such as the PopJam bots automatically doling out "likes") to help them begin to think critically about what they want to interact with.

AGES 9–12

Children in this age range may not only have daily access to a device, but they may even have their own dedicated phone or tablet. It's important to build in healthy habits and conversations before these ages, so your child knows how to handle the increased responsibility and freedom that comes with greater access. Don't ignore that tech is around, but make sure that your child is exploring with safe conditions and that you have discussions about the challenges they encounter.

In addition to vetting each app your child uses, there are a variety of tools to help you monitor your child's activity.

- iOS 12 has a screen-time report which is great for monitoring kids' (and your own) time spent on apps. It's a great way to see how much time your kids are spending and on which apps—and it's a good tool for self-reflection, too.

- Apple ID allows you to customize your protections; you can go into Settings and turn off in-app purchases.
- You can connect third-party apps that give detailed reports on how screen time is being used. Circle (formerly from Disney) is a great product that allows you to connect different devices and see detailed reporting on how screen time is used. It also gives parents the ability to control access and hours of play.
- A fantastic tool, Bark, uses artificial intelligence to recognize acts of cyberbullying, inappropriate posts, and warning signs of depression in your child's usage and behavior. The app can connect across all of your family's devices. It predicts potentially harmful behavior and notifies parents about what interactions to check up on.

Many parents let their children access a wider variety of apps and even social networks at these ages, and it's challenging to let go of the reins and trust that our children are being safe online. That's why Bark and other monitoring tools like it have been developed to bridge the gap between a child's freedom and safety. In an interview with *Forbes*, Bark's CEO Brian Bason described the inspiration behind creating the monitoring app. His description echoes the fear every parent experiences as their kids dive deeper and deeper into the online world:

Despite having spent my entire career in social/mobile technology, I didn't have a clear sense of how best to keep my own kids safe online when they were old enough to have internet-connected devices. I didn't like the idea of spot-checking my kids' devices, which is the default tactic used by most parents. In addition to being time-consuming and invasive, it's a highly ineffective approach to monitoring your child's online activity. In the summer of 2015, I founded Bark to help keep my (and everyone else's) children safer online.[10]

More tools are being developed to help parents, and more research is being done to understand the effect our internet-connected world is having on our kids. Continue to educate yourself on issues of social comparison, validation, and addiction. As your child becomes interested in social interactions, consider how scorecarding behaviors or social pressures may affect them, and talk to them about how these elements might be influencing their actions and their mental health.

AGES 13+

Once you get to the teenage years, it's unrealistic to have the expectation that you'll be able to manage everything your child is doing. By 13, the majority of kids are going to own their own cell phone, be connected, and have the

10   Amit Chowdhry, "How Bark Protects Kids from Online Bullying," *Forbes*, October 31, 2017.

ability to download any app they want. They're also able to get on most platforms legally, per the Terms of Use.

Even outside the world of media, as your child gains more autonomy in the teen years, they're going to be exposed to things you probably won't like as a parent. As a teenager, I went to parties, was exposed to people doing drugs and drinking alcohol, and had to responsibly navigate those situations. Parenting in the age of social media presents the same challenges, and the best we can do is to prepare our children to make good decisions.

I know that when Kaylie starts to get on social media, I won't be right beside her for every interaction. I'm focused on educating her about the issues she'll encounter, such as social validation, addiction, and manipulation that we've covered so far in this book. I want to make sure she knows her values and understands the effects of her interactions, particularly as we see levels of anxiety and depression rise among teens (though as discussed earlier, I don't think we can solely blame tech or social media).

When she's about to post about where she is and what she's doing, I want her to think about whether she needs everyone else to know.

In addition to those concerns, teens also need to be aware of the permanence of social media. With the popularity of Instagram "Stories," increased use of messengers, and an exodus of young people from Facebook, we're seeing some positive indicators that children are trying to tighten up their networks and not put themselves out there quite as much. And for good reason: particularly in their teens, people's reputations on and offline begin to matter.

WHEN THE PAST COMES BACK TO BITE

I've encountered story after story of kids who get into college and lose scholarships, are kicked off teams, or lose jobs because of things from their past that resurface on social media.

In a specific example, someone told me about a young person I'll call Ben, who was fresh out of school and trying to get a job at a well-known investment bank. The position was a coveted one, and the pool of applicants was highly competitive. Ben had a high GPA, an impressive resume, and a well-connected network, and he made it through the first round of the application process. When the bank invited Ben back for a final meeting—where, presumably, he was going to be offered the job—he was unpleasantly surprised to find that someone at the bank had Googled him. They had found social media posts from four or five years prior, in which he'd alluded to doing drugs. He was passed up for the job. The person who told me this story? It was a friend of a senior manager at the bank.

Interestingly, this friend of the manager called the senior manager up to tell him he was being a hypocrite: they'd done their share of keg stands back in the day, after all. But it didn't matter. When the bank stumbled over information about Ben's past, he lost his edge over the other candidates.

Sometimes, these stories unfortunately rise to international notoriety. In June 2019 Kyle Kashuv, a Parkland high school shooting survivor, had his acceptance into Harvard University rescinded because of racist and anti-Semitic remarks he made on text messages and a shared collaborative document with classmates.[11] There is a lot to unpack with these situations, but this is another stark reminder that anything done online potentially goes onto the permanent records of these youths (and adults alike). In this instance, the messages weren't posted on social media, underlining the fact that these issues aren't restricted to open and social platforms.

While Snapchat and Instagram "Stories" have allowed teens to create posts with the "assurance" their content will disappear, it's still possible to grab screenshots. Once

---

11 Patricia Mazzei, "Racist Comments Cost Conservative Parkland Student a Place at Harvard," *New York Times,* June 17, 2019.

we put something out there on social media, there is potential for it to become permanent.

Alongside sex, alcohol, and drugs, social media has become one of the uncomfortable subjects that parents need to talk to their kids about. By beginning these conversations early, we can set the stage to guide them to healthy habits throughout their childhoods.

CONCLUSION

I'll never forget the look in Kaylie's eye when the PopJam bots began to follow her, and I realized the full implications of her life online. Her wide-eyed surprise sparked a new era of my life: that moment inspired me to educate myself, form a company, and write this book. I've gone deeper down this rabbit hole than most, and I'm excited to bring back what I found, to help more kids and parents venture safely into the online world.

The only reason that moment with Kaylie had such an impact—the only reason my company and this book exists—is because I was there. As she has continued to find new apps and pursue new interests, I've been there each step of the way to guide her. When you're exploring apps with your child, you see things that aren't so obvious—in their look, their body language, and the way they engage—that help you understand what they need.

My relationship with Kaylie and our conversations about tech continue to evolve. She's at an interesting age right now where social circles are starting to grow beyond one or two friends and subdivide into little cliques. For me, it's been really interesting to observe that process and the role technology plays in it.

In fact, technology has been fundamental in making sure her relationships continue to thrive: as mentioned earlier, our family moved to a different province a couple of years ago and she adeptly leveraged technology to stay in touch with old friends. When I was a kid, if a friend moved away, you'd never see or hear from them again. Back then, relationships you had would effectively end (ironically until you tracked them down on Facebook decades later).

This is the beautiful side of tech: it connects us. I tend to agree with people like Jordan Shapiro, Diana Graber, and many more who advocate that as parents we have to lean into tech and take an active role in introducing our children to it. I know for me, by better understanding what's going on, I'm able to have more meaningful conversations.

Kaylie and I talk all the time. When she shows an interest

in a platform that makes me uneasy, I'm able to point to examples to show why I'm uncomfortable, and we talk about what that means.

We share in tech together: we recently started coding mods for Minecraft, so she can start to introduce some custom elements into the game she loves so much. She's learning how these programs, apps, and games actually work. It's great, important time that we get to spend together.

Obviously as she gets a little older, we'll discuss more serious things like the permanence of online engagement, social validation, and related topics. By leaning into tech, I forced myself to get educated about the benefits and the challenges. I know that when Kaylie is ready, we'll be prepared for those conversations.

Jordan Shapiro nailed it when he pointed out that we're in a new normal with the developments of tech. This is the world today. It's now up to us as parents to accept it and take a very active role in guiding our children.

There are excellent resources out there, as you've seen throughout this book. Diana Graber, Adam Alter, and Jordan Shapiro all have excellent books on this topic for further reading. Interestingly, those of us working in the space of children and tech cite a lot of the same sources, which signals that there isn't enough research on this subject. The correlation between tech use and rates of depression, anxiety, and suicide is probably more than coincidental, but it's not fully understood. Deeper study needs to be done to learn what the effects of tech truly are, and how we can protect ourselves, and our kids. I hope that as a result of our work we begin to see more studies and more people looking closely at what parents and children can do to engage in safe behavior in the online world.

A CALL TO ACTION

Manipulative screen time and social comparison are two of today's biggest tech-related issues in my opinion, and in light of that, there are steps we can take to better understand the issue as responsible parents.

Right off the bat, do an assessment of what platforms your children are using, and be aware of how social media and gaming companies operate. Most people understand cyberbullying, but behavior like exclusion, tagging people, and accumulating "likes" and followers are lesser known dangers. I want parents to understand social validation and social comparison and that these behaviors could be symptomatic of mental health or anxiety issues.

Parents can use the information presented here to have positive conversations with their kids from their earliest stages of exploration into online media. Even parents with app-savvy teenage kids can open the doors of communication about the challenges they're facing on social media. I hope this book has made you better equipped to have those conversations, ask better questions, and be more aware of things happening under the surface that could potentially be harmful.

In the long run, I want the conversation to continue to grow so that child psychologists and universities can initiate further studies and look more into the effects of tech on our children. Dr. Renae Beaumont, the child psychologist I interviewed for this book, is initiating a study on the impact of tech on kids, and she urges researchers to look into these issues as well. "More research is needed on the influence of technology on children, including longitudinal studies that follow cohorts of children over many years to examine the long-term impact on social, emotional, physical and cognitive development."[1]

Parents, educators, and researchers interested in following the latest research on the effects of screen time can read the latest studies by Common Sense Media (commonsensemedia.org). Another of my advisors, Darren Laur, is doing fantastic work in presenting to hundreds of thousands of school-age children and their parents about digital literacy and responsibility. Darren, also known as

---

1   Dr. Renae Beaumont, personal email communication with the author, March 17, 2019.

the White Hatter, is a retired Staff Sergeant and highly sought-after keynote speaker and expert in social media safety and digital literacy. Extensive resources are available to parents on his website (thewhitehatter.ca).

With more studies and more education, we can continue to push innovations that make platforms better.

There are more positive trends emerging, and the bigger social media platforms are moving in the direction of tighter communities and privacy with less emphasis on amassing "likes" and followers. We are doing our part at Kinzoo as well, working hard to build a private messenger to better serve the needs of families, including younger users.

After all, our children are our future, and they're inheriting an increasingly online world. Let's give them a good one.

ACKNOWLEDGMENTS

I want to start by thanking my wife Heather, who helped immensely through the process of writing this book. She was incredibly helpful in reading drafts, giving feedback, helping me ensure I didn't start getting too nerdy with numbers and giving me quiet time when I needed to research, gather my thoughts and get to writing. Thank you so much—I love you!

Thank you to my two kids, Kaylie and Aiden. Kaylie, thanks for being curious in your exploration of technology. As your dad, I promise that I'll do anything to protect you, and your early experiences made me understand how important it was to educate myself on the role of technology in our family. Thank you also for helping me craft Kinzoo in its early days, and especially for deciding on our mascot, the red panda! Aiden, you are just beginning to explore with technology and your innocence reminds me how important it continues to be to learn and explore for the next wave of children. I love you two more than words can ever express. Children deserve to live in a world where they can get the best that technology has to offer, while avoiding the worst of it.

A special thank you to Dr. Renae Beaumont for writing my foreword, and for contributing so much to the book. I am very careful to not make assertions that I shouldn't make, and your input into the psychological impacts of technology really helped to round out key aspects of the book.

Thanks to Anthony Ly, a talented graphic designer, for all of the amazing graphics you created for the book. I think images help so much in telling a story and you did an amazing job of bringing things to life throughout my book.

As said in the book, more research is needed to fully understand the role of technology in our lives, both positive and negative. But, thank you to the amazing people that have been researching, writing, and speaking about technology and its impact on children and youth. We may not always agree on everything, but it is important that we push the conversation ahead. Thanks to the great work of leaders including Adam Alter, Diana Graber, Jordan Shapiro, Anya Kamenetz, Michelle Borba, and Tristan Harris.

ABOUT THE AUTHOR

SEAN HERMAN is the father of an 8-year-old daughter and a 2-year-old son. The experiences his daughter had online inspired him to start Kinzoo, a private messenger that turns screen time into family time. As Founder and CEO, Sean aims to make Kinzoo the most trusted brand in the world for incorporating technology into our children's lives, and he wants to help parents mold their kids into responsible digital citizens. As a CFA Charterholder, Sean is uniquely qualified to analyze the future of technology from both the consumer and company perspectives. He lives in Vancouver with his two children and wife of twelve years.